The Catholic Biblical School Program

YEAR THREE

OLD TESTAMENT CONTINUED: EXILE AND RESTORATION

TEACHER GUIDEBOOK

Prepared by
Angelo G. Giuliano, Judith A. Hubert, Dorothy Jonaitis, and Brian Schmisek

I0892803

PAULIST PRESS
New York/Mahwah, NJ

The scripture quotations contained herein are from the New Revised Standard Version: Catholic Edition Copyright © 1989 and 1993, by the Division of Christian Education of the National Council of the Churches of Christ in the United States of America. Used by permission. All rights reserved.

Cover design by Sharyn Banks

Book design by Celine Allen

Nihil Obstat: Rev. Msgr. Robert Coerver
Censor Librorum

Imprimatur: + Most Reverend Kevin J. Farrell
Bishop of Dallas

December 29, 2008

The *Nihil Obstat* and *Imprimatur* are official declarations that the work contains nothing contrary to Faith and Morals. It is not implied thereby that those granting the *Nihil Obstat* and *Imprimatur* agree with the contents, statements, or opinions expressed.

Copyright © 2009 by Paulist Press, Inc.

All rights reserved. No part of this book may be reproduced or transmitted in any form or by any means, electronic or mechanical, including photocopying, recording or by any information storage and retrieval system without permission in writing from the publisher.

Permission is granted to teachers of these materials to reproduce for their students "Suggested Answers" and "Unit Tests."

ISBN: 978-0-8091-9589-3

Published by Paulist Press
997 Macarthur Boulevard
Mahwah, New Jersey 07430

www.paulistpress.com

Printed and bound in the
United States of America

Dedication

It is with respect and gratitude that this revision of *The Denver Catholic Biblical School Program* is dedicated to Sister Macrina Scott, OSF. It was her recognition of the need for a serious Bible study for the Catholic laity that led to the creation of the Catholic Biblical School in 1982. As the founder and for twenty years director of the school, Sister Macrina is a leader in the area of adult Catholic biblical literacy. We are grateful to her for the great gift that she has given to the church.

Because of her vision and determination, literally thousands of Catholics have had their eyes and hearts opened to the word and have grown in faith and knowledge, deepening their relationship with God through their study of scripture. With the publication of the Biblical School materials by Paulist Press beginning in 1994, Sister Macrina's dream bore fruit throughout the country. It is our hope that these revisions, renamed *The Catholic Biblical School Program,* will keep that dream alive well into the twenty-first century.

In addition, we would be remiss not to acknowledge the significant contributions of Steve Mueller, PhD, to the development of the original Biblical School program. We also remember Mary E. Ingenthron, now deceased, whose delightful illustrations grace this book.

Contents

Foreword

This teacher guidebook represents the culmination of more than twenty-five years of experience. Sister Macrina Scott, OSF, began the Catholic Biblical School in Denver in 1982 with the support of Archbishop James V. Casey. The program, founded on some of the best Catholic biblical scholarship, was an instant success and quickly grew beyond Denver. In 1994, Paulist Press began publishing the program, making it readily available around the country.

Catholic biblical scholarship reached new heights in the last decades of the twentieth century and has continued to do so into the twenty-first century. This guidebook builds on the solid foundation of the original program with the insights of recent scholarship. Moreover, each of us as authors has grown in knowledge and appreciation gained from teaching, studying, and praying the sacred text. So, together we bring a renewed energy and vigor to the task.

Each author has contributed something unique to the program. Mr. Gene Giuliano, who taught in the Denver program for four years, was a type of Abraham figure when "he got up and went" to Dallas, Texas, moving his wife and daughter from Denver. At that point the Catholic Biblical School in Dallas was merely a dream. Largely because of his efforts, the program established a strong base here and we were able to hire another faculty member the following year.

After teaching in the Catholic Biblical School in Denver for eleven years, Sister Dorothy Jonaitis, OP, left to pursue a doctor of ministry degree. Following her graduation, she accepted a position with the University of Dallas to teach in the fledgling Catholic Biblical School. Her experience in the program and her energetic teaching style were beneficial and led to more growth.

Angeline Hubert had been associate director of the Catholic Biblical School in Denver. As there is a time for all things under the sun, Angeline was ready to assist the Catholic Biblical School at the University of Dallas. Her teaching ability, her attention to detail, and her organizational structure were indispensable. Angeline knew the program inside and out and we benefited greatly from her expertise.

For my part, the opportunity to partner with such dedicated, faith-filled professionals has contributed to my own deepened understanding of the sacred text. When I began at the University of Dallas, I immediately worked to bring this successful program to the "Bible belt." The program's continued success is a testament to those Catholics who desire to know more about the scriptures. I want to thank all those students in the Dallas–Fort Worth area who made this program a reality here. Ultimately, they brought us together.

We are now able to share with you the knowledge, experience, faith, and spirituality of outstanding faculty members in this revision of the teacher guidebook. Know that you are reading a labor of love.

Should any teacher of this program need assistance, please feel free to contact us. Know that we are here for advice, support, encouragement, or simply to share ideas. You can reach us at:

www.udallas.edu/ministry
ministry@udallas.edu

Brian Schmisek, PhD
Dean, School of Ministry
University of Dallas

Introduction

Welcome to the third year of the Catholic Biblical School Program, *Old Testament Continued: Exile and Restoration*. After guiding participants through the first-year journey from Genesis through Kings and the second-year journey with Jesus and the early Christian community, you are a seasoned guide. You are ready to lead the study of the Hebrew prophets, the psalms, and other literature of the exile and restoration.

Throughout the journey it is essential to keep in view the goal, which is to lead participants into an experience of God's word as alive and able to change their lives. By returning regularly to this goal, you will avoid wasting time on the many distracting and discouraging bypaths that offer themselves along the way.

As you know, the four-year plan for this program provides a map by which to guide your course (see page 81). Many years of experience have gone into this arrangement of the books of the Bible and general biblical topics. By following this plan you will ensure that the students' time is used to the best advantage.

Overview of the Third Year

The third year of the program returns to the study of the Old Testament. This journey will take students through the turbulent era from about 750 to 400 BC. During this time both the Northern Kingdom of Israel and the Southern Kingdom of Judah were destroyed, in 722/21 and 587/86 BC respectively and the people were taken off into exile. But since destruction is never the last word of a loving God, the Babylonian exile ended and the people returned to the land.

Amidst these crucial events, a deeper and more mature experience of God emerged as the prophets spoke God's words of judgment and hope, the historians reflected upon the implications of exile and restoration, and the psalmist expressed the spectrum of emotions from praise and exuberance to lament and despair. The people were reminded over and over that God was at work in the everyday social, political, and religious crises that they faced.

Unit One

In the first unit, "Prophecy Before the Exile," students concentrate on the great prophets who exercised their ministry prior to 587/86 BC. Beginning with Amos and Hosea, prophets to the Northern Kingdom, and then moving to Isaiah of Jerusalem, Micah, Zephaniah, Nahum, and Jeremiah, prophets to the Southern Kingdom, students discover how covenant infidelity brought God's judgment. With the threat of destruction and annihilation facing the people, these prophets challenged them to see their lives from God's perspective.

Unit Two

In the second unit, "Exile and Restoration," students concentrate on the message of the exilic prophets and the writings of the early restoration period. After experiencing the pain of the destruction of Jerusalem in the Book of Lamentations and Obadiah's indictment of Edom, the focus shifts to the great prophets of the exile, Ezekiel and Second Isaiah (Deutero-Isaiah). These two men recognized in the midst of the utter hopelessness of their situation an experience of God's saving presence. They re-thought the theology of the LORD and his relationship to his people in new and creative ways. Unit two also includes a study of Third Isaiah, who was active during the time of the return from exile, Haggai and Zechariah, who urged the speedy rebuilding of the temple, and the story of the restoration of the land under the priest Ezra and the governor Nehemiah.

Unit Three

The third unit, "After the Exile," continues the study of the restoration. By reading 1 and 2 Chronicles, students learn how the Jews rewrote their history to meet the needs of the post-exilic community. The prophets Joel, Malachi, and Deutero-Zechariah give further insights into the restoration period. The beautiful Book of Ruth will inspire students with its message of courage, fidelity, and tolerance toward outsiders. Finally, students will turn to a study of the poetic love lyrics in the Song of Solomon (Song of Songs) and the magnificent psalms that express so eloquently the prayer life of Israel.

The third year will be a journey to the center of the Hebrew faith experience—the disaster of exile and the unexpected joy of restoration that formed Judaism. Just as we Christians perceive our faith in the light of the death and resurrection of Jesus, so Judaism perceived its faith in the light of the exile and restoration, which shaped subsequent attempts to express the meaning of Judaism.

As you resume the study of the Old Testament, look for opportunities to point out the connections between the third-year material and what students have previously studied in the Old and New Testaments. The prophets and psalms were especially important for the early Christians, who scrutinized the scriptures for clues to understanding Jesus. Christians found in the prophetic texts insights into Jesus' identity and the meaning of his death and resurrection. Encourage your students to check the cross-references to the New Testament to discover how these passages were used by early Christian authors.

Preparing for the Third Year

In the first two years of the program, the material studied was primarily narratives and letters. Neither form depends much upon poetic expression. This year a large part of the material you will teach is expressed in the meaning-charged form of poetic speech, with the vivid images and parallel construction characteristic of Hebrew poetry. Much of the beauty and power of prophetic speech stems from its poetic character. Students who are unfamiliar with how poetry works will need help in understanding the poetic utterances of the prophets, the Song of Solomon (Song of Songs), and the psalms.

Reading the prophets is also difficult because their message was a response to specific historical events. The message of each prophet was intimately connected to the social and political problems that triggered his oracles. It is important to share the historical background of the prophets with your students. Without making these connections to each prophet's original situation, it is difficult to understand what he intended to say.

Since students are reading and studying for more than mere information, be attentive to the changes in thinking and acting that this material might stimulate. Students may experience discomfort when confronted by the prophets' challenging messages of justice and fidelity.

Use of These Materials

First of all, these materials were developed for groups of adults. One could use the questions for personal study, but the sharing of knowledge and faith by the students is important for their learning. The group process not only bonds the students into communities of learning, but also reinforces the idea that we all learn from one another. Each of us can be a source of insight and encouragement.

This program is most effectively taught by a qualified teacher who has significant background in scripture. The role of the teacher both as knowledgeable instructor and as a facilitator of the experience of scripture study is important. While studies show that adults thrive in self-directed study situations, the instructor can model what it means to be a student of scripture and can act as an on-the-spot resource.

The program includes that often neglected component of so much adult education—homework. Many programs rely solely on reading and discussion and do not assign any homework. When this program started, many people thought that adults would not put up with the demand of weekly homework. Our experience tells us otherwise. Not only have students appreciated their assignments, but they have learned more effectively through their writing. Written homework makes students more responsible in their reading and study of the material. But, more than anything else, the discipline of formulating a written answer compels students to carefully think through their answers. Having a written answer is helpful for the small group discussion. Written answers also encourage the introverts who are often likely to remain quiet in the midst of free-flowing group discussion.

Format for the Weekly Class

A weekly two-hour class is suggested, but the class format can be tailored to the needs of your community. For example, in some areas of the country, the class meets only once a month, with three lessons offered on a Saturday. The weekly class time involves an opening prayer, small group discussion of the homework assignments, a chance to address questions that have arisen, and a lecture by the teacher on the material to be studied for the coming week's lesson. This format provides a good balance between the students' discussion and their listening to the teacher's lecture.

The class time is divided up in this way:

5–10 minutes: Opening Prayer (prepared and led by students on a rotating basis)

5 minutes: Announcements

45–50 minutes: Small Group Discussion (students share written homework answers)

5–10 minutes: Student Questions and General Group Discussion

45–50 minutes: Teacher's Preview Lecture (on material to be studied for the coming week)

At the start of the year, students are assigned to a discussion group of six to eight students. They generally stay in their assigned group for the entire year. Each week, one of the group members acts as the facilitator of the discussion. This experience gives the students a chance to develop some skill in leading a Bible discussion group.

Note that you always lecture on the material that the students will be studying during the coming week. For example, the **Suggested Lecture Topics** under Lesson II.3 should be given to prepare students for Assignment II.3. This preview gives the students an orientation and a context so that they will be able to get the most out of their own reading and study. You can supply much of the background material that students will need for their homework assignment.

At the end of class, you collect the weekly homework assignments and review them. Since the students have worked hard preparing their answers, you ought to take time to carefully review and comment on their papers. As instructor, you should be aware of students who have difficulty interpreting the texts or applying them appropriately with regard to church teaching. It is important to make encouraging comments on the students' papers, but error and inadequate interpretation cannot go unchallenged. Reading the papers each week will take time, but it will enable you to know your students better.

Textbooks are used to supplement careful reading of the biblical texts and are listed at the start of each unit. Although the textbooks are helpful, it is important to stress that the answers to the questions, unless a question specifically states otherwise, are to be found in the Bible and not in commentaries, textbooks, or footnotes.

Basic Principles

There are several underlying assumptions on which this program is based:

1. The entire Bible is inspired and normative for Christian faith. Individual parts must be understood in relation to the whole, not in isolation. As Vatican II's Dogmatic Constitution on Divine Revelation (*Dei Verbum*) reminds us: "God, the inspirer and author of both testaments, wisely arranged that the New Testament be hidden in the Old and the Old be manifest in the New" (§16). The value of studying the entire Bible is that each of us is stretched in new ways by the parts we might not choose to study.

2. Adults need to be actively involved in their learning. The purpose of the lectures is to assist students in their own search for answers. Student opinions and their experiences must be taken seriously as part of the educational process.

3. Scripture addresses the total human person. Therefore, the teaching of it should utilize right-brain and left-brain approaches in as great a variety as possible, using various formats, including:

- Personal study guided by questions
- Group discussion
- Lecture
- Tests
- Creative activities, including art, music, poetry, etc.
- Memorization of verses
- Audiovisual aids

4. Adults deserve the best that scholarship has to offer. Their time is too valuable to be spent reading or listening to outdated information.

Advice for the Teacher

Your most valuable asset in guiding the journey is your own prayerful reflection on scripture. If God's word is alive and active in you, you will be more likely to pass it on to your students as a living word.

A second asset is your knowledge of scripture and, to a lesser extent, of related areas such as church history and theology. The information that you communicate to your students is only a small portion of what you need to know in order to teach effectively. As long as you teach, you need to continue renewing and updating your biblical education. You cannot be content with the basic knowledge that you pass on to your students. You are fortunate if you work on a team or are in contact with peers who can share your study.

Honesty is another essential quality for you as a teacher. Many students want simple, easy answers, but the Bible does not provide them. Instead, it serves as a challenge and guide. Its difficulty is such that on many points there is a wide variety of scholarly opinions. Be honest in recognizing the difficulty and the diversity in the Bible. Do not allow your students to read simply what they want into the text. In the same way, do not impose your own agenda on the biblical text. If you are not honest with the text, you cannot teach your students to be honest with the text.

You also need to understand your students. If you listen to them and read their papers carefully each week, you will come to know each of your students individually. You will find that many of them share these common characteristics of adult Catholic Bible students.

1. They are often unsure of themselves as students, especially as students of the Bible. It is im-

portant that you read their homework papers each week and affirm them for what they have done well, which is usually much more than they realize. If you correct them on matters that have nothing to do with the content of the program, such as grammar and spelling, you run the risk of turning them away from biblical study.

2. They sometimes find it difficult to remember the material taught. It is helpful if you return to major ideas frequently. At every opportunity, review previously studied material by connecting it with new material.

3. Their real interest is often the message of the scripture for their own lives. Help them see that this includes not only their personal and family life but also their parish community, their liturgical experience, and their lives as citizens. Avoid the types of scholarly debates that have little potential for application.

4. They are able to find the meaning of the text for their own lives, and may do so in ways that will surprise you. Many students have reported how powerful a lesson was in enabling them to deal with some personal crisis. Once the word is opened to them, they will find its application. Avoid imposing your interpretations in a way that might stifle their own encounter with the word.

5. They want to be challenged. When this program was planned, many professional educators said that it was much too demanding and that "Catholics aren't ready for anything like this." But, from the beginning, the response has been overwhelming. Individual students may try to evade the requirements and resist their application. But in the end, they will be grateful for the structure. They will know that they have learned more thoroughly than they could have without the requirements of the program.

6. They are able to learn from modern scholarship if it is presented to them carefully, avoiding jargon and controversies that do not really affect the core meaning of a text. It is your responsibility to assimilate the scholarly material and present the consensus as well as the church's teaching on scripture in language that makes it clear and applicable to real life.

Your preparation will enable you to enter into this adventure with enthusiasm. Those who have taught this program have found it among the most challenging and enriching experiences of their lives.

Student Workbook and Teacher Guidebook

This teacher guidebook is meant to be used in connection with the student workbook. It does not reproduce the materials in the student workbook that each student will purchase. You will need to have a copy of the student workbook to familiarize yourself with its format and contents.

For each lesson, the student workbook contains the study objectives, a reading assignment, a geography task, important terms, written work, optional challenge questions, a suggested memory verse, and suggestions for further reading. Some lessons also include exercises. Supplementary Readings are provided at the end of the student workbook and are keyed to various lessons.

For each lesson, the teacher guidebook contains materials specifically for you as teacher. Besides a listing of the assigned readings from the Bible and the textbooks, these include:

Assignment Objectives that focus the material for your presentation.

Rationale for Student Questions that states the purpose of each question that is asked of the students. The numbering in this section corresponds to the written work in the student workbook.

Suggested Lecture Topics that are meant to be suggestions, not an outline of what you present. Every teacher will organize his or her lecture in a unique way. The suggested topics are especially related to the materials in the lesson.

Suggested Answers that are keyed to the student questions. You might wish to copy these answers for the students, or you could make one copy for each group to have during its discussion of the homework assignment. The suggested answers do not attempt to be exhaustive. No answers are provided for questions that ask for the students' opinions or for a creative response. The suggested answers focus the students' attention on the basic information that they can discover in their reading and study, but students will often find different answers to the questions.

Unit Tests that can be duplicated and used to evaluate the students' progress. The unit test provides an opportunity for integration of the assigned materials, assimilation of the basic information that every biblical student should know, and accountability for the content of what has been studied in the unit. The main work of the unit has already been completed when the students turn in their weekly written assignments. The test is not comprehensive, but rather a way to solidify the basic information that the students need to know.

It is hoped that these materials will help you as you lead others to the mystery of The One who is revealed to us through reading and studying the sacred texts. As you have discovered from the work of the previous two years, the journey brings many surprises. Students often begin their study of the prophets with a vague awareness of the meaning of biblical prophecy and the role that the prophets played in the religious experience of Israel. As their study progresses, many students are surprised at how aspects of the prophets' situation are similar to their own. Consequently, the message of the prophets is not experienced as having relevance for the prophets' time only. Rather, the challenge of God's word as the prophets experienced it in their situation once again comes alive for your students. Their encounter with the historic books, the Book of Ruth, Song of Solomon (Song of Songs), and the wonderful Book of Psalms will also enrich their appreciation of the word of God in their lives.

So, with Isaiah we say:

> Come, let us go up to the mountain of the
> Lord,
> to the house of the God of Jacob;
> that he may teach us his ways
> and that we may walk in his paths.
> (Isa 2:3b; NRSV)

UNIT I
Prophecy Before the Exile

Objectives

To enable students to:

1. Describe the historical and social situation in Israel from the eighth century BC to the fall of Jerusalem in 587/86 BC.
2. Explain the basic forms of prophetic speech and the methods by which the prophetic message was handed on.
3. Recognize the prophetic themes of vocation (call), covenant fidelity, social justice, the marriage of God and Israel, and the destruction of the temple.
4. Appropriate and apply the Old Testament prophetic mission and message to contemporary issues.

Textbooks

Primary Text: The Bible. Use a good translation with scholarly notes.

Other Texts: For helpful background and handy reference we recommend:
Eerdmans *Dictionary of the Bible* (cited as EDB)
Hammond's *Atlas of the Bible Lands* (cited as Hammond Atlas)
Lawrence Boadt's *Reading the Old Testament* (cited as Boadt)
Abraham Heschel's *The Prophets* (cited as Heschel)
Thomas L. Leclerc's *Introduction to the Prophets* (cited as Leclerc)

Assignments

Each lesson is to be studied by the students in preparation for their group discussion. For each biblical passage, students are to study the biblical text and footnotes for that particular passage, complete other assigned readings, and do the written work *on a separate page*.

I.1 INTRODUCTION TO THE PROPHETS IN ISRAEL

I.2 AMOS

I.3 HOSEA

I.4 ISAIAH 1–12

I.5 ISAIAH 25, 28–39

I.6 MICAH, ZEPHANIAH, NAHUM

I.7 JEREMIAH 1–6

I.8 JEREMIAH 7–20

I.9 JEREMIAH 21–24, 26–33, 36–38, 52

I.10 UNIT ONE REVIEW

UNIT ONE TEST

I.1 Introduction to the Prophets in Israel

Assignment Objectives

To enable students to:

1. Understand the historical and social factors that contributed to the development of prophecy in Israel.
2. Recall the early prophets covered in the narrative material of the Books of Samuel and Kings studied in the first year of the Catholic Biblical School Program.
3. Recognize the differences between the early prophets and the classical prophets.
4. Describe the characteristics of biblical prophecy.

Read

Boadt, pages 303–15; Heschel, pages xiii–31; "Classical Prophets: Differentia from Early Prophets," #1 in the SUPPLEMENTARY READINGS at the back of the student workbook

Rationale for Student Questions

To enable students:

1. To recognize the nature of the biblical prophet's mission and message and to distinguish the early prophets studied in the first year of the Catholic Biblical School Program from the classical prophets who will be studied this year.
2. To identify characteristics of the prophetic role by reviewing one of the early prophets.
3. To recognize the fact that it might not always be easy to distinguish a false prophet from a true prophet in a context of competing prophecies.
4. To examine Abraham Heschel's claim regarding the connection made in the prophetic message between guilt and responsibility and to apply his assertion to contemporary circumstances.
5. To become acquainted with Abraham Heschel's idea that the prophet is not only aware of ideas about God, but also enters into a sympathetic sharing of God's attitudes or feelings.

Suggested Lecture Topics

- Biblical prophecy and the role of the prophet with particular emphasis on the connection between the word of God spoken by the prophets and the historical situation in which they lived.
- Common assumptions held by ancient Israel about the world (e.g., about the cosmos, causality, time, the individual, and the group).
- The historical and theological significance of events occurring between 750 BC and 400 BC, including the fall of the Northern Kingdom, the fall of the Southern Kingdom, the Babylonian exile, and the restoration of the post-exilic community in their land.
- The connection between God's word and its poetic expression in prophetic speech.
- Introduction to Hebrew poetry as used in prophetic texts, in particular the notion of parallelism.

SUGGESTED ANSWERS FOR UNIT I.1

1. a. The biblical prophet:
   - Speaks the word of God into the current historical situation
   - Participates in the decisions made by God and his angelic advisors and in God's *pathos*
   - Is called by God to lead Israel back to covenant faith
   - Attempts to instill in the people of Israel the conviction that they are not God's people unless they are morally upright
   - Speaks for those without a voice (e.g., the underprivileged, the forgotten, the poor, victims of injustice)

   b. Similarities between the early/former prophets and the classical/latter prophets:
   - Both groups spoke the words of God.
   - Both groups had a strong sense of the tradition of the covenant.
   - Both groups spoke for those without a voice.
   - Both groups held the conviction that in order to be God's people, Israel had to be morally upright.
   - Both groups experienced the spirit of God. (The former prophets experienced the spirit of God rushing upon them, while the latter prophets experienced the spirit of God, in a way not described, as the source of prophetic messages.)

   Differences between the early/former prophets and the classical/latter prophets:

EARLY/FORMER PROPHETS	CLASSICAL/LATTER PROPHETS
There are no accounts of their call stories except in the cases of Samuel and Elisha.	There are several instances of first-person accounts of their call stories.
There are many narratives about their lives and deeds, often colored by imaginative details and touches of folk-tale heroism. There is a much smaller record of their words.	With the exception of Jeremiah, there is very little information about their lives and deeds. There is a much greater record of their words.
Although they understood themselves to be bearers of God's word, they became involved in revolts, coups d'etat, harem intrigues, etc.	They placed greater emphasis on the word of God and did not feel the need to engage in intrigues to bring about change in political policy.
They were members of bands of prophets or prophetic guilds who followed a particular leader.	They acted individually.
There was a greater emphasis on oral prophecies than on written oracles.	There were prophetic schools in which disciples of the prophets collected their oracles in books under the names of individual prophets.
Their activity was marked by psychic gifts of seeing the future, ecstatic behavior, and divination to discover the divine will rather than "messages" to be delivered.	Less emphasis was placed on ecstatic activity/divination. They saw their primary role as challenging popular but false values while exhorting the people to rediscover the covenant and to reverse their evil ways.
They were concerned with discovering the divine will for specific occasions and individuals.	Their prophetic message was spoken to the entire nation.
They were cultic/royal prophets, who were part of the payroll of kings or temples and could be called on for a vision or prediction in moments of need.	They had less association with the cultic element of Israel's life.

5. According to Heschel, the prophet experiences a reflection of and participation in the divine *pathos*—prophetic sympathy with God. The prophet not only has ideas about God but enters into the feelings of God.

I.2
Amos

Assignment Objectives

To enable students to:

1. Identify in their historical and social context the person and message of Amos.
2. Better understand Amos's emphasis on the obligations of covenant life, in particular as they relate to social justice.

Read

Amos 1–9; Heschel, pages 32–46; Leclerc, pages 123–41; "Pre-exilic Prophets: Overview—Amos," #2 in the SUPPLEMENTARY READINGS at the back of the student workbook

Rationale for Student Questions

To enable students:

1. To recognize the prophetic dependence on poetic images rather than abstract ideas to convey their messages.
2. To notice the prophet's emphasis on identifying the people's sinfulness and how it destroys covenant life.
3. To note the characteristics of a prophet exemplified by Amos and how these contribute to their own developing awareness of what a prophet is.
4. To recognize the prophet's appeal to history as a way of reminding the people of their relation to God.
5. To begin to notice the recurring theme of God's relationship to the nations, which discloses something about who the prophet thinks God is and how God is relating to our world.
6. To discover how the biblical prophets and their message might challenge contemporary ways of viewing God and approaching life.

Suggested Lecture Topics

- Historical and social background of the Northern Kingdom of Israel from the splitting of the kingdoms after Solomon until the time of Amos.
- Particular circumstances, most likely under Jeroboam II of Israel, which provoked the responses of Amos (see 2 Kings 14).
- Particular style, theological themes, and social justice concerns of Amos.
- Poetic use of imagery by Amos to communicate his message.

God needs prophets in order to make himself known, and all the prophets are necessarily artistic. What a prophet has to say can never be said in prose.

— Hans Urs von Balthasar, "The Glory of the Lord,"
A Theological Aesthetics

SUGGESTED ANSWERS FOR UNIT I.2

1. a. God:
   - Roars like a lion (Amos 1:2; 3:8)
   - Comes like a fire (Amos 5:6)
   - Punishes injustice among humans, whether Israelites or others (Amos 1; 2; 3:14–15; 4:2–3; 5:11; 6:7–11; 8:9–14)
   - Especially punishes those who are known (Amos 3:2)
   - Crushes like a loaded down cart (Amos 2:13)
   - Relents of planned punishments (Amos 7:3, 6)
   - Shakes Israel among all the nations, as one shakes with a sieve, (Amos 9:9)

2. a. In Amos 5:10–12, the prophet condemns:
   - Resistance to justice and truth
   - Oppression and taxation of the weak
   - Oppression of the just, taking bribes, and rejecting the poor

   In Amos 8:4–6, the prophet condemns:
   - Oppression of the poor
   - Unfair business practices
   - Selling the poor into slavery

   b. Because of the covenant, Israel was to distinguish itself from all the other nations by its compassionate care for the poor, the widow, the orphan, and strangers in their land (see Exod 22:20–22; Deut 24:17). Since in ancient society these groups were powerless, Israel considered the LORD to be their special protector.

3. a. In chapter 7, the following points are made about Amos:
   - He shows his love for the people by interceding for mercy when God threatens them (Amos 7:2, 5).
   - He has made an enemy of the priest Amaziah (Amos 7:10–14).
   - He originally was a herdsman and dresser of sycamores, not a professional prophet (Amos 7:14).
   - He was called from his ordinary work by God and made a prophet to Israel (Amos 7:15).
   - He was not frightened into silence by Amaziah's threats (Amos 7:16–17).

4. a. Within the context of enumerating Israel's acts of injustice and abuse of religious practices, Amos describes the exodus/wilderness experience as one of the great saving acts of God; Amos thereby contrasts God's actions on behalf of Israel with Israel's behavior.

   b. God's acts of judgment against Israel are meant to bring about Israel's repentance. Among other forms of judgment, the LORD sends against Israel plagues similar to those sent against Egypt during the exodus.

   c. Israel's empty religious practices are condemned by God, who claims that offerings and sacrifices were not made during Israel's forty years of journeying in the wilderness, perhaps because such elaborate practices were not necessary.

5. God is in relationship with non-Israelite nations as well as with Israel. God protects and guides them, yet punishes them when they do evil. This revelation by Amos indicates a developing sense of universalism in the thought of Israel.

I.3 Hosea

Assignment Objectives

To enable students to:

1. Describe in their historical and social context the person and message of Hosea.
2. Recognize the major themes of the Book of Hosea, especially the analogy of the covenant with marriage.

Read

Hosea 1–6, 11–14; Heschel, pages 47–50, 53–58, 70–75; Leclerc, pages 142–61; "Pre-exilic Prophets: Overview—Hosea," #2 in the SUPPLEMENTARY READINGS at the back of the student workbook

Rationale for Student Questions

To enable students:

1. To recognize that Hosea is expressing, through concrete images rather than abstract ideas, his own understanding of who God is and what God does.
2. To discover that the Old Testament has often been stereotyped in ways that are not supported by a careful reading of the text.
3. To notice again that the prophets appeal to the formative moments in Israel's history in order to support their message.
4. To build skill in determining the meaning of a prophetic text based on its Old Testament context and to recognize how the text is used in New Testament circumstances.
5. To examine the prophetic use of a particular image of God and to reflect on that image in terms of their own experience of God.
6. To recognize the importance of appropriating biblical texts for their spiritual enrichment.

Suggested Lecture Topics

- Historical events and the social situation in the Northern Kingdom of Israel (ca. 750–722/21 BC) leading to its destruction by Assyria.
- Deuteronomistic version of the fall of Israel to Assyria and the evaluation of this event found in 2 Kings 14–17.
- Deuteronomistic evaluation of Israel's kings.
- Israelite concept of marriage, in particular how it differs from a contemporary understanding of marriage.
- Hosea's use of marriage as an analogy for Israel's covenant relationship with God.
- Conflict between Yahwism and ancient fertility cults honoring the Baals and the significance of this conflict in the development of the idea of the LORD as a creative source of life.

SUGGESTED ANSWERS FOR UNIT I.3

1. a. Hosea compares God to:
   - A husband (Hos 2:16 [2:18 NAB and NJB])
   - A parent (Hos 11:1)
   - A lion, a leopard (panther NAB), and a bear (Hos 11:10; 13:7–8)
   - An accuser in a legal case (Hos 12:2 [12:3 NAB and NJB])
   - The dew (Hos 14:5 [14:6 NAB and NJB])
   - A shade tree (Hos 14:8 [14:9 NAB and NJB])

   b. According to Hosea, God has the following feelings:
   - Tenderness, love (Hos 2:19 [2:21 NAB and NJB]; 11:4)
   - Love and anger in conflict (Hos 11:8–10)
   - Compassion and love (Hos 14:3–4 [14:4–5 NAB and NJB])

2. a. Examples of Hosea portraying God as a God of justice include:
   - Hosea 5:1–15
   - Hosea 6:4–11
   - Hosea 11:5–7

   b. Examples of Hosea portraying God as a God of love include:
   - Hosea 2:14–23
   - Hosea 11:1–4, 8–11
   - Hosea 14:4–9 (14:5–10 NAB and NJB)

3. According to Hosea, the exodus/wilderness experience of Israel was one of complete dependence on God, who acted not only as a deliverer but also as a provider. In the deliverance of Israel from Egypt, God was revealed as savior, as the only God for Israel, and as the one who provided for Israel to the point of satisfaction. However, according to the prophetic text, when Israel is satisfied the people grow complacent and turn from God.

5. a. In Hosea's description, God:
   - Loved and called the child (Israel)
   - Cared for the child (Israel) by instructing, healing, and showing affection
   - Gave direction and provided for the child (Israel)
   - Corrected the child (Israel) when necessary, while still loving and showing the child (Israel) compassion

---

The distinguishing feature of the prophets... was not so much their clear vision of the future as their accurate perception of the present. God revealed the meaning of their contemporary situation in order that they might show their people that continuing in their present choices would be destructive, and that it was possible to choose differently and thereby avoid disaster.

— D. Bergoffen, *"The Apocalyptic Meaning of History,"* The Apocalyptic Vision in America

I.4 Isaiah 1–12

Assignment Objectives

To enable students to:

1. Describe in their historical and social context the person and message of Isaiah of Jerusalem.
2. Recognize that Isaiah's call experience is the key to his prophetic career.
3. Explain major themes of Isaiah, in particular the holiness of God and the hope for a royal Davidic messiah.

Read

Isaiah 1–12; Heschel, pages 76–94, 112–14; Leclerc, pages 162–74; "Pre-Exilic Prophets: Overview—Isaiah," #2 and *The Jewish People and Their Sacred Scriptures in the Christian Bible*, §21, #3 in the SUPPLEMENTARY READINGS at the back of the student workbook

Rationale for Student Questions

To enable students:

1. To be aware of the prophetic critique of worship and connect this awareness with the proper attitude toward worship today.
2. To notice how Isaiah uses images rather than abstract concepts to envision a world where God's word is heard and acted on and to encourage students to express concretely their vision of such a world.
3. To reflect on Isaiah's distinctive experience and understanding of God as revealed in his call story and to recognize the importance of this view in the celebration of the Eucharist.
4. To build skill in determining the meaning of a prophetic text based on its Old Testament context and to recognize its use in New Testament circumstances.
5. To connect a prophetic text to a Christian understanding of it through the church's liturgical use of the text.
6. To examine a prophetic text from the perspective of a later understanding of it.

Suggested Lecture Topics

- Social, political, and historical situation in Judah from the death of Uzziah to the reign of Ahaz (742–715 BC) as the background for the problems that provoked the early oracles of Isaiah (see 2 Kings 15–16).
- Structure and composition of the Book of Isaiah.
- Theological emphases that surface in Isaiah 1–12, for example:
  - Holiness of God
  - Covenant fidelity
  - Failure of leadership in Judah
  - God's threat of judgment and promise of deliverance
- Literary pattern that characterizes biblical call stories, emphasizing the role of Isaiah's call story for understanding his vocation.
- Notion of *holiness* as the ancient Hebrews understood it, in particular its unique quality as distinctive of God.
- Later Catholic understanding of the gifts of the Spirit (Isa 11:2–3).
- Concept of the fuller sense of the biblical text (*Sensus Plenior*).

SUGGESTED ANSWERS FOR UNIT I.4

1. a. In regard to the worship offered by the people, God:
    - Does not care about it, has had enough of it, and takes no delight in it (Isa 1:11)
    - Had not asked for sacrifices (Isa 1:12)
    - Considers the offerings futile and the incense an abomination (Isa 1:13)
    - Hates the festivals and is weary of them (Isa 1:14)
    - Will not listen to the people's prayers (Isa 1:15)

2. a. Isaiah's vision of a peaceful world is a world that is unified in the single worship of God and in submission to God's instruction and judgment (Isa 2:2–4). All nations shall flow to the mountain of the house of God, which will be raised above the hills; from Zion shall go forth the law and from Jerusalem the LORD's word (Isa 2:2–3). Also, resources will be used for peace, not war (Isa 2:4), and weapons will be turned into farming/gardening implements (Isa 2:4).

3. a. In Isaiah's vision the holiness, glory, and majesty of God are emphasized. As transcendent king, God exercises divine power over all the earth (Isa 6:1–3, 5). Also, God has the authority to call someone, in this case Isaiah, to a prophetic mission (Isa 6:8–10).
   b. The church uses Isaiah 6:3 in the acclamation that concludes the thanksgiving (i.e., the Preface) part of the Eucharistic Prayer.

4. a. Some possibilities that have been offered:
    - Hezekiah, the son of Ahaz
    - Isaiah's son (see Isa 8:1–4)
    - A faithful king who will replace Ahaz
    - A child to be born after the threat from Syria and Israel has disappeared—a time when "God with us" can be proclaimed

   b. At a much later date, Matthew quotes Isaiah 7:14 as a fulfillment passage to support his belief that Jesus is the son of David, the son of a virgin, and the presence of God among God's people. Matthew understands the sign of deliverance given to Ahaz as being fulfilled in a transcendent way in a fuller sense (*Sensus Plenior*) in the conception and birth of Jesus.

6. a. The messiah:
    - Is a descendant of Jesse, and so is a descendant of David (Isa 11:1)
    - Is filled with the spirit of the LORD; the spirit of wisdom, understanding, counsel, might, knowledge, and fear of the LORD (Isa 11:2)
    - Judges the poor with righteousness and decides for the meek with equity (Isa 11:4)
    - Is righteous and faithful (Isa 11:5)

   b. The reign of the messiah is characterized by:
    - Peace and harmony
    - The dissolution of the roles of predator and prey
    - The absence of fear, danger, violence, destruction, and pain
    - The earth being full of the knowledge of the LORD

The text [Isaiah 6] makes clear in exemplary fashion what prophetic visions were considered to be, according to the prophets' own interpretation. They do not tell of seeing forces beyond this world. What they claim is a profound vision, a seeing into the depths of the one human and divine reality, a reality in which earth and heaven, far from cleaving apart, belong together in an inseparable unity. A fourth dimension opens up beyond everyday perception.

— *Klaus Koch,* The Prophets

I.5 Isaiah 25, 28–39

Assignment Objectives

To enable students to:

1. Describe more fully in their historical and social context the person and message of Isaiah.
2. Recognize major themes from the Book of Isaiah, especially the themes of trust in God and the idea of the remnant of Israel (Isa 37:31–32).
3. Describe the siege of Jerusalem by the Assyrian King Sennacherib in 701 BC and contrast the biblical interpretation of this event with that of the Assyrians.

Read

Isaiah 25, 28–39; Heschel, pages 94–112; Leclerc, pages 174–87; "The Prism of Sennacherib, iii 18–49," #4 in the SUPPLEMENTARY READINGS at the back of the student workbook

Rationale for Student Questions

To enable students:

1. To examine the use of a particular literary form and its impact on the meaning of the biblical text.
2. To recognize the dependence on poetic images to convey prophetic messages and to evaluate the meaningfulness of these images in light of their own personal experience.
3. To connect a prophetic text to a Christian understanding of it through the church's liturgical use of the text.
4. To recognize that every text expresses a point of view (i.e., the same event when reported for different reasons produces a different understanding of the meaning of the event).
5. To recall that there was no belief in a meaningful life after death during Isaiah's time and to encourage students to reflect on their own thoughts and feelings about death.

Suggested Lecture Topics

- Social, political, and historical events during the reign of Hezekiah of Judah (see 2 Kings 18–20) that provide the stimulus for Isaiah's oracles.
- Literary text as an expression of a particular point of view, which in turn directs the selection, editing, and presentation of events.
- Structural similarities in composition between the earlier oracles of Isaiah to Ahaz (Isaiah 6–8) and Isaiah's oracles to Hezekiah.
- Isaiah as a model of the prophetic vocation.
- Theological emphases in Isaiah 25, 28–39.
- Poetic imagery and parallelism used by biblical prophets and their contribution to doing theology.

SUGGESTED ANSWERS FOR UNIT I.5

1. Examples of passages in Isaiah 25 that give hope and comfort to those in crisis include:
   - God has proven to be faithful and sure in the past, accomplishing divine plans against ruthless peoples and being a stronghold for the poor and needy (Isa 25:1–5).
   - God will make a feast for all peoples on the mountain of the LORD (Isa 25:6).
   - The LORD will destroy death forever, wipe away tears from all faces, and remove from all the earth the reproach of God's people (Isa 25:8).
   - The LORD will again prove to be a savior for God's people (Isa 25:9–12).

2. a. In Isaiah 31, God is compared to a lion (Isa 31:4) and to hovering birds (Isa 31:5).

   b. God is like a lion who is unperturbed by the puny shouts of the shepherds because their noise poses no threat to his power. God's ways are not thwarted by our feeble human attempts to alter those ways. God is like hovering birds that protect their young against danger. So the LORD will protect the chosen people against the threats of nations who wish to harm them.

4. a. The only difference between the account in 2 Kings and the account in Isaiah is that 2 Kings describes events prior to the Rabshakeh's arrival at Jerusalem. These events include the capturing of Judah's fortified cities by Assyria, the demand for tribute, and Hezekiah's agreeing to pay the tribute. While not appearing in Isaiah, these events are found in the Prism of Sennacherib version. The principal difference between the biblical accounts and that of the Prism of Sennacherib is that the Assyrian account does not describe Hezekiah consulting with Isaiah, Hezekiah's prayer, God's promise to thwart Sennacherib's efforts, the killing of 185,000 in the Assyrian camp by the angel, and the return home of the Assyrian king where he is killed as was prophesied. Instead, the Assyrian account describes only a totally successful Assyrian campaign culminating in the "caging" of Hezekiah in his royal residence in Jerusalem and his paying the demanded tribute.

5. a. In Isaiah 38:18, Hezekiah describes the gloominess of the netherworld, a place where those there can neither praise nor thank God. Moreover, there is hopelessness in that they do not hope for the faithfulness of the LORD.

The Destruction of Sennacherib

By George Gordon, Lord Byron

The Assyrian came down like the wolf on the fold,
And his cohorts were gleaming in purple and gold;
And the sheen of their spears was like stars on the sea,
When the blue wave rolls nightly on deep Galilee.

Like the leaves of the forest when Summer is green,
That host with their banners at sunset were seen;
Like the leaves of the forest when Autumn hath blown,
That host on the morrow lay withered and strown.

For the Angel of Death spread his wings on the blast,
And breathed in the face of the foe as he passed;
And the eyes of the sleepers waxed deadly and chill,
And their hearts but once heaved, and forever grew still.

And there lay the steed with his nostril all wide,
But through it there rolled not the breath of his pride;
And the foam of his grasping lay white on the turf,
And cold as the spray of the rock-beating surf.

And there lay the rider distorted and pale,
With the dew on his brow and the rust on his mail;
And the tents were all silent, the banners alone,
The lances unlifted, the trumpets unblown.

And the widows of Ashur are loud in their wail,
And the idols are broke in the temple of Baal;
And the might of the Gentile, unsmote by the sword,
Hath melted like snow in the glance of the Lord!

I.6 Micah, Zephaniah, Nahum

Assignment Objectives

To enable students to:

1. Set in their historical, political, and social contexts the persons and prophetic messages of Micah, Zephaniah, and Nahum.
2. Recognize the major themes and theological contributions of Micah, Zephaniah, and Nahum.

Read

Micah, Zephaniah, Nahum; Heschel, pages 124–29; Leclerc, pages 188–204, 212–26; "Pre-exilic Prophets: Overview—Micah, Zephaniah, Nahum," #2 in the SUPPLEMENTARY READINGS at the back of the student workbook

Rationale for Student Questions

To enable students:

1. To examine the use of Micah 5:2 (5:1 NAB and NJB) in Matthew's gospel and to reflect on why this verse would have significance for New Testament Christians.
2. To build skill in determining how a prophetic text might have meaning for the contemporary world.
3. To recognize the importance of failed leadership for covenant infidelity.
4. To connect a prophetic text to a Christian understanding of it through the church's liturgical use of the text.
5. To reflect on the message and theology of the Book of Nahum.
6. To evaluate the appropriateness of a particular biblical perspective for today.

Suggested Lecture Topics

- Social, political, and historical events during the period between Isaiah and Jeremiah in which Micah, Zephaniah, and Nahum prophesied.
- Structure and major theological themes of Micah, Zephaniah, and Nahum.
- Themes shared with other prophets, for example:
    - Remnant
    - Day of the LORD
    - God's justice and deliverance
    - God's rule over the nations

SUGGESTED ANSWERS FOR UNIT I.6

1. a. In Matthew 2:6, the chief priests and the scribes use this passage to indicate where the messiah is to be born. Also note that John 7:42 alludes to this passage from Micah among other texts to reach the same conclusion.

   b. David was born in Bethlehem and anointed king there.

3. a. Zephaniah condemns officials and judges (Zeph 3:3), prophets and priests (Zeph 3:4).

   b. The officials are described as "roaring lions," the judges as "evening wolves." Therefore, both groups are condemned for preying on those who are vulnerable. The prophets are reckless and faithless in the exercise of their ministry. The priests have profaned what is sacred and have done violence to the law.

Prophecy is essentially a ministry of disclosure, a stripping bare. Israel's great prophets do not merely lift the veil of the future in order to destroy false expectation; at the same time, they expose the conduct of their contemporaries. They do so in a way that brings into full view the secret motivations and concealed intentions behind what these people are doing. Prophets tear the masks away and show the true face of the people behind them. Among these kinds of prophets, Micah is one of the greatest in his penetration of camouflage. He sees two groups of people as being most intensively concerned with the art of masquerading: the political authorities and the public representatives of religion and piety.

— *Hans Walter Wolff,* Confrontations with Prophets

I.7
Jeremiah 1–6

Assignment Objectives

To enable students to:

1. Describe in their social, political, and historical contexts the person and message of the prophet Jeremiah.
2. Recognize the importance of Jeremiah's call and early oracles in understanding his prophetic work.
3. Characterize the poetic style and imagery used by Jeremiah.

Read

Jeremiah 1–6; Heschel, pages 130–46; Leclerc, pages 235–42, 251–55; "Pre-exilic Prophets: Overview—Jeremiah," #2 in the SUPPLEMENTARY READINGS at the back of the student workbook

Rationale for Student Questions

To enable students:

1. To reflect upon the biblical theme of call and to see its relationship to their own experience.
2. To detect images of idolatry used by Jeremiah and to evaluate the effectiveness of those images today.
3. To identify with the people of Jerusalem at a particular moment in their history.
4. To recognize the range of meanings that the image of circumcision can evoke in different times, places, and circumstances.
5. To make a personal connection with the biblical text.

Suggested Lecture Topics

- Social, political, and historical situation in Judah during the time of Josiah and the Deuteronomic reform, in particular the time when the oracles in Jeremiah 1–6 were most likely proclaimed (627–621 BC).
- Contents, history of composition, major themes, and connections of the Book of Jeremiah to the prophetic and the Deuteronomic traditions.
- Poetic style of Jeremiah, in particular his use of imagery (e.g., the marriage analogy, war/peace, wound/sickness, and lie/truth).

SUGGESTED ANSWERS FOR UNIT I.7

1. a. According to the call story in Jeremiah 1:4–10, the prophet's mission:
   - Is part of God's plan
   - Is a mission to the nations, to whomever God sends Jeremiah
   - Is to speak whatever God commands Jeremiah to speak
   - Entails the double task of destruction and building up as seen in his oracles of judgment and his oracles of salvation
   - Will be very difficult, but will be sustained by God

2. a. Some images Jeremiah uses for idolatry:
   - The ancestors of the house of Israel went after worthlessness (Jer 2:5).
   - The ancestors of the house of Israel defiled God's land and made God's heritage an abomination (Jer 2:7).
   - Israel's prophets went after things that did not profit (Jer 2:8).
   - God's people have changed their glory for that which does not profit (Jer 2:11).
   - God's people have hewn out cisterns for themselves, broken cisterns that can hold no water (Jer 2:13).
   - Long ago Israel broke their yoke, burst their bonds, and said "I will not serve!" On every high hill and under every green tree Israel sprawled and played the whore (Jer 2:20).
   - Israel has become a wild vine (Jer 2:21).
   - Israel is like a restive young camel and a wild ass in heat, lustful, and sniffing the wind (Jer 2:24).
   - Israel is like a wicked woman seeking lovers (Jer 2:33).
   - Israel is like a woman who has played the harlot with many lovers (Jer 3:1–2, 6, 8).
   - Israel is like a faithless son (Jer 3:22).

4. a. Israel's understanding of circumcision was somewhat like our Christian understanding of sacraments (i.e., an outward sign of the internal dedication to God and the covenant people). Both Jeremiah and Paul stress that the external sign of circumcision without the inner motive is essentially worthless.

The prophet is guided, not by what he feels, but rather by what God feels. In moments of intense sympathy for God, the prophet is moved by the pathos of God, Who is disillusioned by His people. The state is far from being his main concern. His declarations are made from the point of view of God. It is rarely a personal, direct reaction to a situation, and mostly an articulation of God's view and an identification with it. Yet, in taking God's part he defends the people's position, since in truth God's pathos is compassion. For compassion is the root of God's relationship with man.

— *Abraham J. Heschel,* The Prophets

I.8 Jeremiah 7–20

Assignment Objectives

To enable students to:

1. Describe the historical, social, and political events during the reign of Jehoiakim of Judah (609–596 BC) that provide the context for the oracles in Jeremiah 7–20.
2. Explain Jeremiah's personal anguish as a prophet in service to the word of God.
3. Recognize the characteristic theological themes of Jeremiah as he proclaims the destruction of Judah.
4. Notice the importance of symbolic actions as a way of communicating the prophetic message.

Read

Jeremiah 7–20; Heschel, pages 146–60; Leclerc, pages 243–51, 255–56, 258–60, 263–65

Rationale for Student Questions

To enable students:

1. To appropriate the message of Jeremiah about misplaced confidence in God and apply it to a modern context.
2. To reinforce previous information about the Deuteronomic authors and their distinctive theological emphases.
3. To learn about the prophet Jeremiah, his relationship with God, and how his theology is expressed through his laments.
4. To respond creatively to a prophetic text.
5. To reflect on Jeremiah's message and to apply it to their own situation.

Suggested Lecture Topics

- Social, political, and historical events from the death of Josiah in 609 BC through the reign of Jehoiakim (609–597 BC) that provoked the oracles of the prophet in Jeremiah 7–20 (see 2 Kgs 23–24).
- Symbolic meaning of the temple for the Jewish people and how its existence was related to their covenant relationship with God.
- How Jeremiah expressed his theology concretely through poetic imagery often drawn from his everyday experiences, symbolic actions, and personal prayers rather than through abstract categories.

SUGGESTED ANSWERS FOR UNIT I.8

2. Deuteronomic themes in Jeremiah 11:1–12 include:
   - Centrality of the covenant provisions and curses for not heeding them (Jer 11:3)
   - The LORD's deliverance of Israel from Egypt (Jer 11:4)
   - God's command to listen and obey (Jer 11:4)
   - The land of promise described as a land of milk and honey (Jer 11:5)
   - The people's infidelity or acts of idolatry (Jer 11:10)
   - The impotence of false gods (Jer 11:12)

3. In Jeremiah's laments the following become apparent: his intimate relationship with God, his total acceptance of the prophetic mission and its consequences, his desire for God's word to be fulfilled and for the wicked to bear God's judgment, and his anguish and pain.

   a. In Jeremiah 11:18–12:6, the prophet:
      - Asks for God's vengeance against the wicked who seek to do the prophet harm and who say that God does not see what they are doing
      - Complains to God that the wicked prosper

   b. In Jeremiah 15:10–21, the prophet:
      - Sees himself as a man of strife and contention to all the land
      - Reminds God that he accepted the prophetic mission and that he has done all that God has asked him to do
      - Claims that he bears reproach because he has done what God has told him to do
      - Asks God to take vengeance for him on his persecutors
      - Sees God as the source of his unceasing pain

   c. In Jeremiah 17:14–18, the prophet:
      - Praises God
      - Asks God to fulfill the prophetic message so that he might be healed and saved, and that his persecutors, not he, may be confounded and broken

   d. In Jeremiah 18:18–23, the prophet:
      - Complains to God that he receives evil for all the good he has done
      - Asks God not to forgive or forget what the wicked have done and are planning to do
      - Pleads with God to act in judgment against the wicked

   e. In Jeremiah 20:7–13, the prophet:
      - Claims that God has deceived him and, as a result, he has become a laughingstock
      - Complains that the prophetic message brings reproach and derision
      - Speaks of his desire to end his prophetic mission and of the fact that he cannot because of the fire within his heart
      - Expresses confidence in God as his support and as a warrior to take vengeance upon his enemies
      - Praises God for delivering the life of the needy from the hand of evildoers

   f. In Jeremiah 20:14–18, the prophet:
      - Curses the day on which he was born and the one who announced his birth to his father
      - Wishes he had not been born, that he had died in his mother's womb
      - Laments his life, which is filled with sorrow, pain, and shame

5. a. As a potter has a purpose for his creation, so too, God has a purpose for Israel. However, it is possible that the final product is not what the potter had in mind, so he may choose to reuse the clay, giving it a new shape. Israel is described as clay in the hands of the LORD. So, God may choose to reshape the divine attitude toward Israel, depending on Israel's response. If God declares salvation for Israel, but Israel turns away, the declaration will be reshaped into judgment. If God declares judgment against Israel and Israel repents, the declaration will be reshaped into salvation.

Catholic exegesis does not claim any particular scientific method as its own. It recognizes that one of the aspects of biblical texts is that they are the work of human authors, who employed both their own capacities for expression and the means which their age and social context put at their disposal. Consequently, Catholic exegesis freely makes use of the scientific methods and approaches which allow a better grasp of the meaning of texts in their linguistic, literary, socio-cultural, religious and historical contexts, while explaining them as well through studying their sources and attending to the personality of each author. Catholic exegesis actively contributes to the development of new methods and to the progress of research.

What characterizes Catholic exegesis is that it deliberately places itself within the living tradition of the Church, whose first concern is fidelity to the revelation attested by the Bible. Modern hermeneutics has made clear, as we have noted, the impossibility of interpreting a text without starting from a "pre-understanding" of one type or another. Catholic exegetes approach the biblical text with a pre-understanding which holds closely together modern scientific culture and the religious tradition emanating from Israel and from the early Christian community. Their interpretation stands thereby in continuity with a dynamic pattern of interpretation that is found within the Bible itself and continues in the life of the Church. This dynamic pattern corresponds to the requirement that there be a lived affinity between the interpreter and the object, an affinity which constitutes, in fact, one of the conditions that makes the entire exegetical enterprise possible.

All pre-understanding, however, brings dangers with it. As regards Catholic exegesis, the risk is that of attributing to biblical texts a meaning which they do not contain but which is the product of a later development within the tradition. The exegete must beware of such a danger.

— *Pontifical Biblical Commission,* The Interpretation of the Bible in the Church *(1993), III*

I.9 Jeremiah 21–24, 26–33, 36–38, 52

Assignment Objectives

To enable students to:

1. Describe the social, political, and historical events (i.e., events that took place during the reign of Zedekiah and led to the Babylonian exile) that formed the background for Jeremiah 21–24, 26–33, 36–38, and 52.
2. Recognize the distinctive emphases of Jeremiah concerning the destruction of Jerusalem and exile as well as glimmers of hope, in particular his prophecy of a new covenant.

Read

Jeremiah 21–24, 26–33, 36–38, 52; Heschel, pages 160–77; Leclerc, pages 242–43, 256–57, 260–63, 265–72

Rationale for Student Questions

To enable students:

1. To recognize Jeremiah's insistence on Judah's destruction and how it might be received by Judah's king at that time.
2. To make connections, as the early Christians did, between the life of Jeremiah and that of Jesus.
3. To examine a biblical theme and its applicability for their own lives.
4. To build skill in determining the meaning of a prophetic text based on its Old Testament context and to recognize its use in New Testament circumstances.
5. To describe the effect the prophet Jeremiah has had on them and to possibly use Jeremiah as a model for their own relationship to God.

Suggested Lecture Topics

- Social, political, and historical situation in Judah during the reign of Zedekiah (597–587 BC) that led to the destruction of Jerusalem and the temple in 587/86 BC and the beginning of the Babylonian exile (see 2 Kgs 24–25).
- What the destruction of the temple meant to the people of Judah, in particular the questions it raised about God's relationship to the people.
- Ancient ideas concerning the king's role in the stability and well-being of the community and in the community's relationship with God.
- Distinctive theological themes the prophet expresses in Jeremiah 21–24, 26–33, 36–38, 52, in particular his hope for restoration.
- Connection between Jeremiah 21–24, 26–33, 36–38, 52 and his commission "to build and to plant" (see Jer 1:10).

SUGGESTED ANSWERS FOR UNIT I.9

2. Both enraged the religious authorities by their preaching in the temple. Both were turned over by the religious authorities to the secular authorities for trial (Matt 27:1–2; Mark 15:1; Luke 19:47; 20:1—2, 20; 22:2, 52–53; 23:1; John 18:19–24, 28).

4. a. According to northern traditions, Rachel, the favorite wife of Jacob, was buried near Ramah in the territory of Benjamin (see 1 Sam 10:2). As a symbolic mother of Israel, she is portrayed by Jeremiah as weeping for her children who "are no more" (Jer 31:16), that is, those of the Northern Kingdom who went into exile. But the LORD comforts her by declaring that "...they shall come back from the land of the enemy; there is hope for your future...your children shall come back to their own country" (Jer 31:16c–17). Weeping should cease and there is reason for hope because Rachel's children, those who went into exile, shall return to their homeland. This passage fits Jeremiah's vision of the future restoration of both Israel and Judah.

   b. Matthew sees Rachel's sorrow and the tragedy of her lost children as described by Jeremiah fulfilled at the time of Jesus' infancy in the slaughter of the innocents. By quoting only part of the prophecy, Matthew refocuses the meaning of the passage. Jeremiah emphasizes that mourning and weeping should cease because the children are not lost; they will be restored. However, Matthew's emphasis is on the mourning and weeping that accompany the loss of the children.

Amos, Hosea, Isaiah, Jeremiah, and Ezekiel were prophets of the presence. Their visions are alive with shattering memories of glimpses of infinity, while the aesthetic quality of their individual styles points to the interpenetrative process by which poetic expression was initiated and sustained. The burden of the great prophets' "office" was the burden of the word which had privately been forced upon them. They subordinated their entire lives to the intrusion of the presence.

— *Samuel Terrien,* The Elusive Presence

I.10 Unit One Review

Students will be responsible for:

1. A memory verse from one of the prophets that they studied during this unit, indicating the translation used and citing the reference.

2. The information included in the following SUPPLEMENTARY READINGS at the back of the student workbook:

   #2. "Pre-exilic Prophets: Overview"

   #5. "Self-Quiz: Mid-Unit One"

   #6. "Self-Quiz: Unit One Maps"

3. Demonstrating familiarity with the chronology of major events and people studied during this unit. Students do not need to know dates, but must be able to chronologically order major events and characters. (For example, Isaiah of Jerusalem came *before* Jeremiah; Zedekiah came *after* Ahaz.)

Suggested Lecture Topics

- Integration of the persons, places, events, themes, and terms connected with biblical prophecy before the exile.
- Geographical, social, and historical situations in which the pre-exilic prophets proclaimed God's word to the people.
- Map exercises as above on map quiz.

YEAR THREE
UNIT ONE TEST

Name ______________________________

Center ________________ **Group #** _____

1. Match the following statements with the appropriate prophet (a prophet's name may be used more than once):

   Amos, Hosea, Isaiah of Jerusalem, Micah, Zephaniah, Nahum, Jeremiah

   ____________ a. married a harlot

   ____________ b. had his scroll burned by King Jehoiakim

   ____________ c. named a child "a remnant shall return"

   ____________ d. proclaimed the birth of Immanuel

   ____________ e. hoped for a new covenant

   ____________ f. urged Judah to surrender to Babylon

   ____________ g. used a good example of a covenant lawsuit

   ____________ h. stressed the Davidic Covenant and the greatness of Mt. Zion/Jerusalem

   ____________ i. during his call, experienced the holiness of God in a vision in the temple

   ____________ j. remained celibate as a sign of the impending end of Jerusalem

   ____________ k. saw God as lover, faithful spouse, and parent

   ____________ l. saw God's justice in the destruction of Nineveh

   ____________ m. connected universal destruction with the proclamation of the Day of the LORD

   ____________ n. rebuked the people in a sermon at the temple

   ____________ o. came from Judah, but called for justice in Israel

   ____________ p. looked forward to a ruler/messiah from Bethlehem

   ____________ q. spoke of woundedness and healing

   ____________ r. named a child "not my people"

2. In his call, Jeremiah is commissioned "to pluck up and to pull down, to destroy and to overthrow, to build and plant." Describe how his prophetic words and ministry fulfilled this commission.

3. Which prophet do you think has the most significant message for the church today? Why?

4. What is the most significant thing that you learned from this unit's study of the prophets?

5. Chronology: In the blank between the columns, write whether the item in the first column came BEFORE or AFTER the item in the second column.

a. Fall of the Northern Kingdom	______________	Fall of the Southern Kingdom
b. Josiah	______________	Hezekiah
c. Amos	______________	Jeremiah
d. Zephaniah	______________	Isaiah of Jerusalem
e. Nahum	______________	Hosea
f. Ahaz	______________	Zedekiah
g. Exile	______________	Exodus
h. Siege of Jerusalem by Sennacherib	______________	Death of Josiah
i. Assyrian Empire	______________	Babylonian Empire

6. Write your memory verse from this unit. Be sure to cite the book, chapter, verse, and translation used.

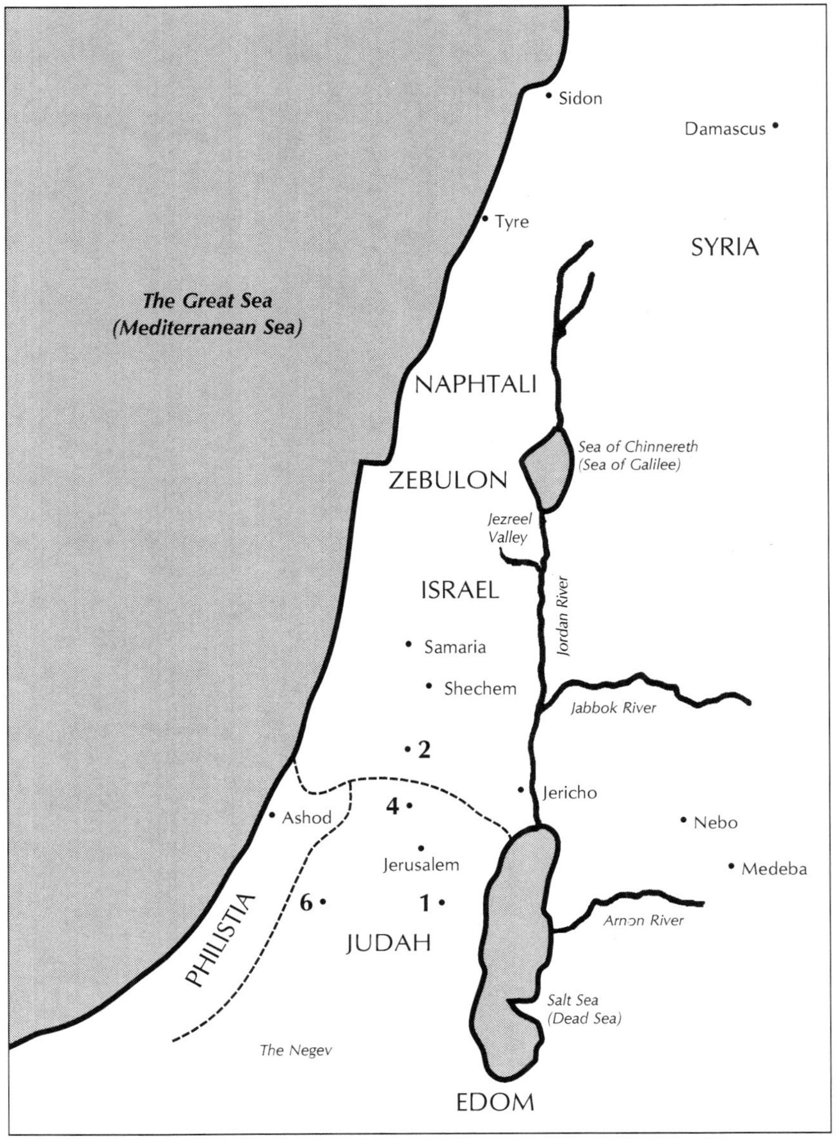

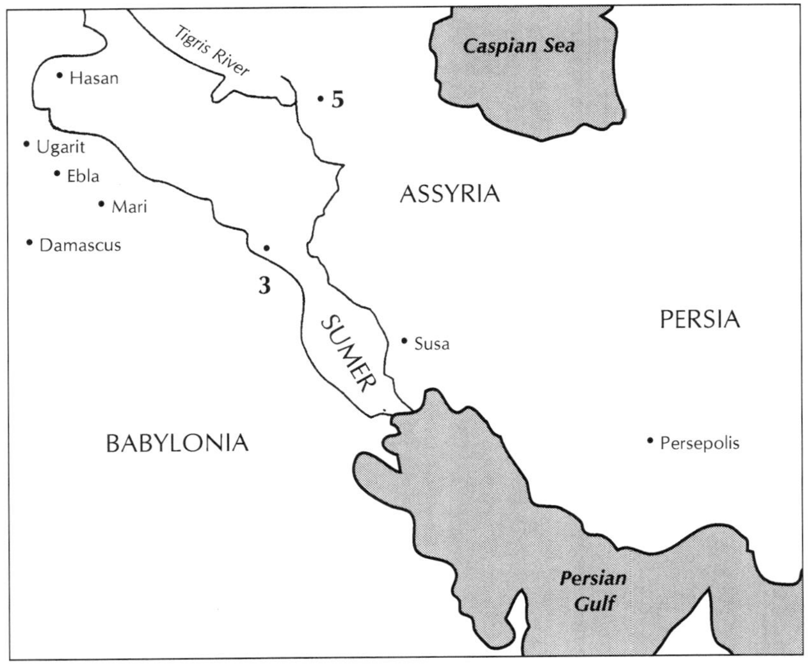

7. Map Test: In the blank next to each place name, write the number of the location on the maps.

_____ a. Anathoth

_____ b. Babylon

_____ c. Bethel

_____ d. Moresheth

_____ e. Nineveh

_____ f. Tekoa

ANSWERS TO YEAR THREE–UNIT ONE TEST

1. Identification of Prophets

a. Hosea
b. Jeremiah
c. Isaiah
d. Isaiah
e. Jeremiah
f. Jeremiah
g. Micah
h. Isaiah
i. Isaiah
j. Jeremiah
k. Hosea
l. Nahum
m. Zephaniah
n. Jeremiah
o. Amos
p. Micah
q. Jeremiah
r. Hosea

5. Chronology

a. Before
b. After
c. Before
d. After
e. After
f. Before
g. After
h. Before
i. Before

7. Map Test

a. 4
b. 3
c. 2
d. 6
e. 5
f. 1

UNIT II
Exile and Restoration

Objectives

To enable students to:

1. Describe the historical and social situation of Israel during its exile in Babylon.
2. Explain the various theologies that arose from the experiences of exile and return.
3. Recognize the prophetic message of the post-exilic prophets and its implications, especially for the New Testament.
4. Identify the impact of post-exilic theology on the writings of Ezra and Nehemiah.
5. Describe the development of Israel as a community built upon the word during the exile and around the rebuilding of the temple after the return from exile.

Textbooks

Primary Text: The Bible. Use a good translation with scholarly notes

Other Texts: For helpful background and handy reference we recommend:
Eerdmans *Dictionary of the Bible* (cited as EDB)
Hammond's *Atlas of the Bible Lands* (cited as Hammond Atlas)
Lawrence Boadt's *Reading the Old Testament* (cited as Boadt)
Collegeville *Commentary on Ezekiel, Daniel* (cited as Collegeville Commentary)
Abraham Heschel's *The Prophets* (cited as Heschel)
Thomas L. Leclerc's *Introduction to the Prophets* (cited as Leclerc)

Assignments

Each lesson is to be studied by the students in preparation for their group discussion. For each biblical passage, students study the biblical text and footnotes for that particular passage, complete other assigned readings, and do the written work *on a separate page*

II.1 LAMENTATIONS, OBADIAH

II.2 EZEKIEL 1–5, 8–12, 16–17

II.3 EZEKIEL 18–24, 33–37, 43:1–12, 47:1–12

II.4 ISAIAH 40–48

II.5 ISAIAH 49–55

II.6 HAGGAI, ZECHARIAH 1–8

II.7 ISAIAH 56–66

II.8 EZRA 1:1–11, 3:1—10:17

II.9 NEHEMIAH 1–2, 4–6, 8–10, 13

II.10 UNIT TWO REVIEW

UNIT TWO TEST

II.1 Lamentations, Obadiah

Assignment Objectives

To enable students to:

1. Describe the historical situation surrounding the destruction of Jerusalem and the temple (587/86 BC) and the response of those remaining in the city.
2. Identify the structure, composition, style, and theological themes of the Book of Lamentations and the Book of Obadiah.
3. Explain the literary pattern and theological significance of the lament as a Jewish poetic device.
4. Begin to recognize the central importance of the destruction of Jerusalem and the exile in the experience of the Jewish people.

Read

Lamentations, Obadiah; Leclerc, pages 272–77; EDB articles: "Acrostic" and "Lament"; "The Meaning of Exile," #7 and "Literature of the Exile: Overview—Lamentations and Obadiah," #8 in the SUPPLEMENTARY READINGS at the back of the student workbook

Rationale for Student Questions

To enable students:

1. To describe the distinctive view of God in the Book of Lamentations.
2. To recognize the way the Jewish people tried to cope with the destruction of the temple by seeking causes for the disaster.
3. To note how they are affected by their reading of lament poems.
4. To discover the message of the Book of Lamentations for those who suffer.
5. To determine the meaning of a biblical book in terms of its original context and how that meaning might be applied today.

Suggested Lecture Topics

- Historical events surrounding the destruction of the temple and the beginnings of exile.
- Social, historical, and theological significance of the Jerusalem temple for Judaism.
- Theological problems that arose for the Jewish people because of the profound, world-shattering experience of the loss of the temple.
- Relationship between Lamentations and Jeremiah.
- Literary pattern and characteristic emphases of the lament form as used by the Hebrew poets.
- Poetic dependence on graphic and concrete imagery to convey a message.
- Explanation of acrostic and the Book of Lamentations as a complete acrostic.
- Obadiah's oracles against other nations.
- Application of laments to current events.

SUGGESTED ANSWERS FOR UNIT II.1

1. There are many answers; a few possibilities are:
   - God became angry at Jerusalem (Lam 1:12c, 13a; 2:1, 3, 22b; 3:1; 4:11).
   - God carried out a threat from long ago (Lam 2:17).
   - God destroyed all of Jerusalem (Lam 2:2, 5b, 8, 17).
   - God silenced the prophets (Lam 2:9c, 14c).
   - In spite of all the failings of Israel, God is still steadfast, merciful, compassionate, and loving (Lam 3:22–26, 31–32, 56–57).

2. a. The author of Lamentations blames the kings (Lam 2:6c, 4:12), the priests (Lam 1:19b, 2:20c, 4:13a), the prophets (Lam 2:14, 2:20c, 4:13a), the princes (Lam 4:8, 5:12), the elders (Lam 4:16b, 5:12), the people themselves (Lam 1:5, 1:18, 1:22), "my lovers" (Lam 1:19), and the ancestors (Lam 5:7).

4. a. There are many possibilities, both positive and negative; some of these might include:
   - God is angry and has made the people suffer because of their transgressions (Lam 1:5b; 2:1).
   - The people are to remember the "precious things that were hers in days of old" (Lam 1:7a).
   - God is steadfast and merciful (Lam 3:22).

5. a. The prophet Obadiah is proclaiming judgment against Edom because its people mistreated their "brother Jacob" (Ob 10) by rejoicing when Judah was conquered and even looting it (Ob 13). Perhaps Edom is a type of "all the nations" (Ob 15) and this means judgment upon all the nations that have mistreated Israel. The reference to Mount Zion might refer to the future glory of Jerusalem and the house of Jacob when Jacob will triumph over Edom (Ob 17–21).

The paradox is that for readers to be challenged, disturbed, scared, spiritually prodded, emotionally battered by a book in no way precludes their taking pleasure in what the writer has wrought—the resonance and shapeliness of the language, the vividness of the realization of the scene, the moral subtlety of represented motives and action and relationships.

— Robert Alter, The World of Biblical Literature, *pages 9–10*

II.2
Ezekiel 1–5, 8–12, 16–17

Assignment Objectives

To enable students to:

1. Describe the social, political, and historical events of the Babylonian exile, in particular as they relate to the person and message of the prophet Ezekiel.
2. Recognize the way Ezekiel expresses his theological message, in particular through the description of his call and his use of imagery, allegories, and symbolic prophetic actions.
3. Identify the structure, composition, and characteristic themes of the Book of Ezekiel.
4. Explain the literary form of allegory and its interpretation.

Read

Ezekiel 1-5, 8-12, 16-17; Collegeville Commentary on Ezekiel 1-5, 8-12, 16-17; Leclerc, pages 278-95; "Literature of the Exile: Overview—Ezekiel," #8 in the SUPPLEMENTARY READINGS at the back of the student workbook

Rationale for Student Questions

To enable students:

1. To identify essential characteristics of Ezekiel's theology.
2. To ascertain the similar and distinctive elements of the call stories in the prophetic texts and to more fully understand the person of Ezekiel.
3. To recognize the importance of symbolic actions as a form of prophetic expression.
4. To develop the skill of interpreting an allegory.
5. To explore the significance of the destruction of Jerusalem and to give some thought to a contemporary event that could have similar significance.

Suggested Lecture Topics

- Call of Ezekiel.
- Historical, social, and political events surrounding the exile, with mention of who went into exile and when they went.
- Life in Babylon, including the problems that arose for the exiles in relation to their religious lives.
- Structure and composition of the Book of Ezekiel.
- Theological themes that emerged as a result of the exilic experience.
- Characteristic themes found in the Book of Ezekiel, including discussion of how Ezekiel's message relates to the problems facing his community.
- Style of Ezekiel's visions, images, allegories, and symbolic actions as ways of relaying the message of God to the people.

SUGGESTED ANSWERS FOR UNIT II.2

2. a. Similarities between Ezekiel 1:28—3:27 and Jeremiah 1:4–19 include:
   - Both are to be prophets to Israel/Judah in judgment against them (Ezek 2:3–4; Jer 1:16).
   - Both have visions (Ezek 1:28; Jer 1:11–13).
   - Both are told not to be afraid of the people (Ezek 2:6a; Jer 1:8).
   - Both receive God's own words (Ezek 3:1–4a; Jer 1:9).

   Differences between Ezekiel 1:28—3:27 and Jeremiah 1:4–19 include:
   - Jeremiah questions his call (Jer 1:6–7), but there is no questioning in Ezekiel.
   - Ezekiel has a vision of the glory of the LORD (Ezek 1:28), but Jeremiah's visions are of "a branch of an almond tree" and "a boiling pot, tilted away from the north" (Jer 1:11–13)
   - The call story indicates that Jeremiah is consecrated before he is born (Jer 1:5), but there is no parallel in Ezekiel.

   Similarities between Ezekiel 1:28—3:27 and Isaiah 6:1–13 include:
   - Both have visions of the Lord on a throne: Ezekiel sees "the likeness of the glory of the LORD (Ezek 1:29) and Isaiah sees "the LORD seated on a throne, high and lofty" (Isa 6:1a).
   - Both hear a voice (Ezek 11:28b; Isa 6:8).
   - Both are told that the people will not understand (Ezek 3:7; Isa 6:9–10).
   - When Ezekiel eats the scroll, he will be worthy to proclaim woe to the people (Ezek 2:8b–9); when Isaiah is cleansed of his "unclean lips," he is told that his sin has been blotted out (Isa 6:6–7).

   Differences between Ezekiel 1:28—3:27 and Isaiah 6:1–13 include:
   - Isaiah says that he is inadequate (Isa 6:5a) but Ezekiel doesn't.
   - Ezekiel bears responsibility for the people not being converted (Ezek 3:18, 20b), but Isaiah is not made responsible.

3. a. In Ezekiel 4, the prophet:
   - Plays war, using a brick as Jerusalem, and sets an iron plate between himself and the city (Ezek 4:1–3)
   - Lies on his left side for 390 days, then on his right side for 40 days (Ezek 4:4–8); he is then told specifically what to eat and drink for 390 days (Ezek 4:9–17)

   In Ezekiel 5, the prophet cuts off his hair and destroys it in various ways (Ezek 5:1–4).

   In Ezekiel 12, the prophet:
   - Prepares an exile's baggage and, in the sight of the people, brings it out by day and digs through a wall in order to carry the baggage out at night (Ezek 12:2–7)
   - Eats bread with quaking, and drinks water with trembling and with fearfulness (Ezek 12:17–18)

   b. The meaning of Ezekiel 4 is that the prophet bears the punishment of Israel (Ezek 4:5b), the people are unclean among the nations (Ezek 4:13), and the people will waste away under their punishment (Ezek 4:17b).

   The meaning of Ezekiel 5 is that Jerusalem has rebelled against the ordinances of the LORD and become wicked (Ezek 5:6). Because of this, God will execute judgment against the people (Ezek 5:8) and scatter those who survive (Ezek 5:10). Nations will taunt and mock Israel (Ezek 5:15a).

The meaning of Ezekiel 12 is that the rebellious house might understand (Ezek 12:3c) because the prophet's action is a sign to them (Ezek 12:6c). They will go into captivity (Ezek 12:11b) and some will die (Ezek 12:13c). Some, however, will escape, tell of their abominations, and then realize that God is the LORD (Ezek 12:16). The land of Israel will become desolate because of their violence (Ezek 12:19c). Every prophetic vision will be fulfilled and there will be no false vision (Ezek 12:23b–24, 27).

4. a. In the allegory in Ezekiel 17:
   i. The first eagle is Nebuchadnezzar.
   ii. The top branch is Jehoiachin.
   iii. The vine is Zedekiah.
   iv. The second eagle is Egypt.

He [Ezekiel] has none of Isaiah's powerful eloquence, none of the human emotion that seems to make Jeremiah so much more directly accessible. Instead, this prophet with his priestly background has a special sense that Yahweh, despite the blows he is inflicting on his people, which at first glance appear so harsh, is in the process of revealing himself not just to this people, but to the entire world of the nations…

In his entire ministry, this prophet is a figure who takes the message of judgment proclaimed by the pre-exilic literary prophets and crowns their work by expressing it in the most uncompromising terms; by forcing Israel to face this confrontation with its God, he also helps Israel to survive the catastrophe of death and go forward toward new life.

— *Walter Zimmerli,* Old Testament Theology in Outline

II.3
Ezekiel 18–24, 33–37, 43:1–12, 47:1–12

Assignment Objectives

To enable students to:

1. Describe more fully in their historical and social context the person and message of Ezekiel.
2. Recognize specific themes from the Book of Ezekiel, in particular Ezekiel's understanding of God's holiness, individual responsibility, and the hope of restoration for the community after the exile.

Read

Ezekiel 18–24, 33–37, 43:1–12, 47:1–12; Collegeville Commentary on Ezekiel 18–24, 33–37, 43:1–12, 47:1–12; Leclerc, pages 295–303; EDB article: "Shepherd"

Rationale for Student Questions

To enable students:

1. To recognize an important change in the understanding of God's justice and the shift from communal responsibility to individual responsibility.
2. To explore the meaning of a prophetic allegory and to critique its contemporary relevance.
3. To learn how the actions of a prophet are related to the prophetic message.
4. To note the meaning of an image used by Ezekiel and see how the image is carried forth into the New Testament.
5. To identify the message of hope in a prophetic text and its relevance for their own lives.

Suggested Lecture Topics

- Ezekiel's use of the traditions of the people, with emphasis on their sinful past.
- Theme of individual responsibility in Ezekiel and its connection to Jeremiah 31:29–30.
- The theme of individual responsibility as carried over into the teaching of Jesus and Christianity.
- Nature of hope and restoration in Ezekiel, especially its relationship to the holiness of God.
- Arrangement of the Book of Ezekiel into texts of judgment, oracles to nations, and hope for the restored community.
- Ezekiel's use of restoration images.

SUGGESTED ANSWERS FOR UNIT II.3

1. a. According to Ezekiel 18 and 33:10–20:
    - Intergenerational responsibility is no longer applicable (Ezek 18).
    - Conversion is possible if one turns away from sin (Ezek 18:21–22; 33:12–16); neither the state of righteousness nor the state of wickedness is necessarily permanent.
    - The way of the LORD is not unfair/unjust, even though people might think it is (Ezek 18:25; 33:20)
    - God derives no pleasure from the death of the wicked (Ezek 33:11a).

2. a. The following are described:
    - Israel's sojourn in Egypt (Ezek 23:3)
    - The divided kingdom (Ezek 23:4c)
    - Israel's alliance with Assyria, worship of idols, and destruction (Ezek 23:5b–8, 10, 33b)
    - Judah's alliance with Assyria (Ezek 23:12–13)
    - Judah's alliance with Babylon (Ezek 23:14–21)
    - Babylon's destruction of Jerusalem and the exile of Judah (Ezek 23:22–31)

3. a. Ezekiel was not to mourn the death of his wife as a sign that the people were not to carry on a mourning ritual when the temple was destroyed and their children were killed (Ezek 24:21–23a). Instead, they were to "pine away" in their iniquities and "groan to one another" (Ezek 24:23b).

   b. Ezekiel was silent so that he wouldn't reprove the people (Ezek 3:26b). When he regains his ability to speak, he will be a sign to them that God is the LORD (Ezek 24:27b).

4. a. According to Ezekiel 34:
    i. The sheep without a shepherd are scattered, they become "food for all the wild animals," and they wander "over all the mountains" (Ezek 34:5–6).
    ii. God will rescue the sheep (Ezek 34:10c), search for the sheep that are lost (Ezek 34:11–12, 16), bring them into their own land and feed them (Ezek 34:13b–14, 27b, 29), and be their shepherd (Ezek 34:15). David will be appointed to continue to shepherd them and a covenant of peace will be made with them so that they will be a blessing (Ezek 34:23–26). However, they will be judged by how they act (Ezek 34:17, 20, 22b).

   b. Parallels between
    i. Ezekiel 34 and Matthew 25:31–46:
       - Both texts speak of judgment by whether they are sheep or rams/goats (Ezek 34:17; Matt 25:32–33).
       - Both texts make reference to blessing (Ezek 34:26; Matt 25:34b).
       - Judgment is based on action, especially action with regard to those who are weak/injured, etc. (Ezek 34:1–4; Matt 25:42–43).
    ii. Ezekiel 34 and John 10:1–18
       - Both passages refer to good shepherds (God/Jesus) who will care for the sheep (Ezek 34:11–16; John 10:11).
       - Both refer to bad sheep and the consequences of their actions (Ezek 34:1–10; John 10:1, 5, 8, 10a, 12–13).

5. a. These things are promised and give hope:
    - Israel will be repopulated, fruitful, and purified (Ezek 36:8, 24–25).
    - The people will have a new heart and spirit (Ezek 36:26).
    - Ruins will be rebuilt (Ezek 36:33–37).
    - The people will return to Israel (Ezek 37:12–14).
    - Israel and Judah will be reunited (Ezek 37:15–22).
    - There will be a new David (Ezek 37:24).
    - The people will remain in Israel forever (Ezek 37:25).
    - God will make a covenant of peace that is everlasting (Ezek 37:26).
    - God's sanctuary will be there forever (Ezek 37:26c–28).
    - The plan for the holy temple will be given to them (Ezek 43:11–12).
    - The glory of the Lord will fill the temple (Ezek 43:5).
    - God will reside with the people because Israel will no longer defile God's name (Ezek 43:7, 9b).
    - Every creature will live in the water flowing from the new temple; trees will line the banks of the river and they will bear fruit for food and healing (Ezek 47:9, 12).

It is staggering and reprimanding and liberating to hear said, "Not for your sake, but for the sake of my name" (Ezek 36:22). All our feverish self-justification is set in perspective... Newness, one learns as one moves from Ezekiel 36 to the dry bones of 37, is not merely another church priority. In this society paralyzed by nuclear issues, shamed by battered women and children, beset with survival issues, newness is wrought out of God's holiness. Newness comes only from God, who will give it in God's own freedom. That may be psychologically ambiguous and sociologically problematic, but theologically and pastorally the claim is clear and hope-filled. Our lives are set back in perspective. For the times when we cannot say with Jeremiah, "It is because I yearn for you," we may hear with Ezekiel, "not for your sake, but for mine." The load is lifted. We begin again. The bones rattle. The air stirs. We could be on our way back home to our true community.

— *Walter Brueggemann,* Hopeful Imagination: The Prophetic Voices in Exile

II.4
Isaiah 40–48

Assignment Objectives

To enable students to:

1. Describe the social, political, and historical events surrounding the end of the exile in Babylon that provide the background for the oracles of Second Isaiah.
2. Recognize the major themes of Second Isaiah, especially the homecoming as a new exodus, images of God as creator, redeemer, and the only God (monotheism).
3. Identify the structure, composition, and literary forms of Second Isaiah.
4. Explain the reasons for distinguishing First Isaiah (Isa 1–39) from Second Isaiah (Isa 40–55).

Read

Isaiah 40–48; Leclerc, pages 304–32; EDB articles: "Cyrus" and "Monotheism, Ancient Israel"; "Literature of the Exile: Overview—Second Isaiah," #8 in the SUPPLEMENTARY READINGS at the back of the student workbook

Rationale for Student Questions

To enable students:

1. To recognize the importance of creation imagery as a way to convey the significance of the end of the exile and the emergence of monotheism.
2. To explain Second Isaiah's connection of theology to political events and to make a correlation with our own time.
3. To recognize the appeal to Israelite history as an aid to understanding the significance of their present experience.
4. To identify the developing emphasis in Jewish theology of God as the only God because idols are not gods at all.
5. To highlight the significance of Second Isaiah as a source for the New Testament authors.
6. To identify with the exile experience.

Suggested Lecture Topics

- Call of the author of Second Isaiah.
- Social, historical, and religious situation surrounding the ending of the exile.
- Structure and composition of the Book of Isaiah and the scholarly conclusion that Isaiah 1–39 and Isaiah 40–55 have different authors.
- Characteristic imagery, theological themes, and historical allusions found in the poetic oracles of Second Isaiah.
- Oracles of salvation as a literary form.

Second Isaiah gives his people a remarkable gift. He gives them back their faith by means of articulating the old story. He gives them the linguistic capacity to confront despair rather than be surrounded by it. And he creates new standing ground outside the dominant consciousness upon which new humanness is possible. A cynic might argue that nothing has really changed. But prophets are not magicians. Their art and calling is only with words that evoke alternatives, and reshaped hardware will not overcome despair in any case. That will come only with the recognitions that life has not been fully consigned to us and that there is another who has reserved for himself his sovereign freedom from us and for us.

— *Walter Brueggemann,* The Prophetic Imagination

SUGGESTED ANSWERS FOR UNIT II.4

1. a. Passages portraying God as creator: Isaiah 40:21–22, 25–26, 28; 41:4; 42:5; 43:1, 7; 45:7, 12, 18; and 48:13.

   b. God, who created the world, has power over everything (Isa 40:26, 42:5, 45:12). God is first and will be the last (Isa 41:4). God, the holy one, has no equal (Isa 40:25, 45:18).

2. a. Cyrus is a victor from the east (Isa 41:2, 46:11a) ("north" [Isa 41:25]) who has been summoned by God into service to save the people of Israel (Isa 41:2–3). Cyrus is God's shepherd and anointed one (Isa 44:28, 45:1a) and is called to trample on rulers and subdue nations (Isa 41:25, 45:1b). Cyrus will rebuild Jerusalem and set God's people free (Isa 45:13). The LORD loves Cyrus and will give him strength to conquer Babylon (48:14b–15).

3. a. The *new* Exodus is the specific subject in these passages:
   - There is a highway in the wilderness (Isa 40:3–4).
   - The "glory of the LORD" is revealed (Isa 40:5).
   - God transforms the wilderness/desert by giving water to all (Isa 41:17–20; 43:19, 20b; 44:3a; 48:21).
   - The people sing a new victory song in the desert (Isa 42:11).
   - The community passes through the waters and the fire (Isa 43:2).
   - God makes a way through the seas and causes chariots and horses to lie down (Isa 43:16–17, 19b).

4. By using satirical writing, the writer sharpens the contrast between the God of Israel and the gods of "the nations." Idols are the work of human hands (Isa 40:19–20, 41:6–7, 44:11a); they are shameful and nothing (Isa 44:9). Those who work on the idols become hungry and thirsty and their strength fails them (Isa 44:12). After he finishes the idol, the worker bows down and worships it (Isa 44:15b, 17, 46:6). The idol-maker does not comprehend what he is doing and the idol he made is an abomination, a fraud, and it cannot "save anyone from trouble" (44:18–20, 46:7).

5. a. John the Baptist is identified as herald of the new age begun by Jesus (Matt 3:3; Mark 1:3; Luke 3:4–6); in John's gospel, the Baptist actually says "I am the voice…" (John 1:23).

   b. There is a warning to the rich of the insecurity of their life despite their wealth (James 1:10) and the author of 1 Peter uses Isaiah to remind the community that their rebirth in Christ is the result of God's creative word (1 Pet 1:24).

   c. Matthew identifies this passage of Isaiah as fulfilled in Jesus (Matt 12:18–20).

   d. Romans 14:11 uses Isaiah to remind us that we who like to judge others negatively will indeed be judged by God. In Philippians 2:10, the role of judge switches to the now exalted Christ Jesus. Isaiah is used in Hebrews to show that there is none greater than God, who "swears by himself" rather than by another (Heb 6:13).

II.5 Isaiah 49–55

Assignment Objectives

To enable students to:

1. Describe more fully the characteristic emphases and theology of Second Isaiah as they relate to the historical and social situation of his audience.
2. Recognize important theological themes from Second Isaiah, in particular the Servant of the LORD and the New Jerusalem, as well as to note the use of these themes by early Christian authors.

Read

Isaiah 49–55; Heschel, pages 184–201; EDB article: "Servant of the LORD, Second Isaiah"

Rationale for Student Questions

To enable students:

1. To analyze the Servant Songs in order to explore the identity of the Servant.
2. To connect two passages in the Old Testament about a loving God and to ponder the significance of these passages for their own understanding of God.
3. To investigate the theme of suffering as redemptive.
4. To recognize the significance of texts from Isaiah used in the liturgy.
5. To make connections between the exile and their own lives.

Suggested Lecture Topics

- What the Jewish people learned about God and themselves from the exile.
- Prophetic use of historical themes to present God's new actions for salvation.
- The exiles' powerlessness and need for liberation from Babylon.
- The Servant as model for participation in salvation.
- Themes of the Servant Songs.
- Various interpretations of the identity of the Servant in the Jewish and Christian traditions.
- Influence of the Servant Songs on the evangelists, especially Mark.
- Role of suffering.

SUGGESTED ANSWERS FOR UNIT II.5

1. a. Evidence from the four Servant Songs supporting the conclusion that:
   i. The Servant is an individual:
      - He is called from the womb (Isa 49:1, 5a).
      - The prophet is speaking as an individual (i.e., Isa 49:1–6; 50:4–9).
      - Isaiah 53 seems to imply an individual sufferer.
   ii. The Servant is the personification of Israel:
      - The Servant is identified as Israel (Isa 49:3 as used in Isa 41:8–9; 44:1–2, 21).
      - Light to the nations (see Isa 2:2–4) is a common designation for the mission of Israel (Isa 49:6b).
      - The one despised is a reference to Israel in exile (Isa 49:7b, c).

> **Note**: The boundaries between the individual and the collective are often quite fluid in the scripture texts, since the head of a group or family embodies the honor of the family. Important individuals frequently represent the entire group (e.g., Jacob, Ephraim, Moses, David, or any king for his nation.)

   b. Some New Testament texts that reflect the fuller Christian sense include:

   For Isaiah 42:1–4:
   - Jesus is the fulfillment (Matt 12:18–21).
   - Jesus is the chosen one in whom God delights (Matt 3:17; Mark 1:11; Luke 3:22a and 23:35).
   - Jesus receives the Spirit (Matt 3:16; Mark 1:10b; Luke 3:22a).

   For Isaiah 49:1–7:
   - Jesus is called/named in the womb (Matt 1:21–23; Luke 1:26–35).
   - Jesus is a light to the nations (Matt 4:16; Luke 2:32; John 1:4).
   - God is glorified in Jesus (John 13:31).

   For Isaiah 50:4–11:
   - Jesus speaks to the weary (Matt 11:28–30).
   - Jesus is beaten and insulted (Matt 26:67 and 27:28–31; Mark 14:65 and 15:15–20; Luke 22:63–65).

   For Isaiah 52:13—53:12:
   - Jesus bears our infirmities and diseases (Matt 8:17).
   - Jesus suffers for us and bears our sins though he has no deceit in his mouth and we like sheep go astray (1 Pet 2:21–25).
   - Jesus suffers silently (Matt 27:12; Luke 23:9).
   - Jesus suffers unjustly (Luke 23:47).
   - Jesus' tomb is with the rich (Matt 27:57–60).
   - Jesus is lifted up (John 12:32–33).
   - Jesus willingly accepts suffering and is hence exalted (Phil 2:7–9).
   - Philip identifies the Servant as Jesus (Acts 8:32–35).

2. a. In both Isaiah and Hosea, God is portrayed as a parent who cannot forget a child, who will not punish forever. God's actions are tender and parental (Isa 49:15; Hos 11:3–4).

4. The Easter Vigil celebrates new life with images of fire, light, and water. Also prominent is the proclamation of the word in which the story of Israel's covenant relationship with God is related and the covenant relationship with the Christian community is affirmed. The Easter Vigil is the celebration of redemption through Jesus the Christ. The catechumens are called to the transforming waters of baptism, sealed with the Spirit, and invited to the banquet of the Eucharist. The people are reminded of their baptismal vows and are invited to speak them with those to be baptized. Given the above, some possibilities for the appropriateness of the readings for the Easter Vigil are:
   - Just as God offered redemption to Israel (Isa 54:5b, 8b), so the Christian community celebrates redemption through Jesus the Christ
   - Just as Israel was called to remember God's constant love and compassion (Isa 54:6–8, 10), so the baptized witness to conversion in their lives.
   - Just as the exiles were called to the saving waters and the rich food that satisfies (Isa 55:1–2), so the catechumens are called to baptism and Eucharist.
   - The Noah story has traditionally been associated with the sacrament of baptism (Isa 54:9).
   - Those baptized join a community that seeks God (Isa 55:6).
   - Just as Isaiah announced that God's word would go forth and not return empty (Isa 55:10–11), so the proclamation of the word at the Easter Vigil bears fruit in the community.

It takes a little historical imagination, however, to understand how radical and incredible the proclamation of the restoration of Israel was. Other nations which fell under the Assyrian and the Babylonian military machines did not survive. Israel, in the theology of Second Isaiah, survived because it had a mission.

— *John L. McKenzie,* A Theology of the Old Testament

II.6 Haggai, Zechariah 1–8

Assignment Objectives

To enable students to:

1. Identify the historical and social context of the return of the exiles and the ways in which they tried to restore their religious beliefs and practice.
2. Describe the person and message of Haggai and First Zechariah and their prophetic contribution to the rebuilding of the Jerusalem temple.

Read

Haggai, Zechariah 1-8; Leclerc, pages 333-46; EDB articles: "Darius, #1," "Satan," and "Zerubbabel"; "Restoration Literature: Overview—Haggai and Zechariah," #9 in the SUPPLEMENTARY READINGS at the back of the student workbook

Rationale for Student Questions

To enable students:

1. To reflect on the restoration experience and its application to the church in the twenty-first century.
2. To discover prophetic messages conveyed through imaginative visions.
3. To note the use of the prophet Zechariah by John of Patmos.
4. To identify the role of the Satan figure in the Old Testament and compare it to contemporary notions of Satan.
5. To explore post-exilic prophecy through a study of Zerubbabel.

Suggested Lecture Topics

- Historical, political, and social circumstances surrounding the return from the exile, in particular the significance of rebuilding the Jerusalem temple.
- Structures and patterns of religious life that characterize pre-exilic and post-exilic Judaism.
- Structure, composition, characteristic imagery, and theological themes found in the prophets Haggai and Zechariah.
- Role of Haggai and Zechariah in the rebuilding of the temple.

SUGGESTED ANSWERS FOR UNIT II.6

2. a. The LORD will restore Jerusalem and the temple (Zech 1:7–17).

   b. The powers that humbled and scattered Judah will have the same done to them (Zech 1:18–21 [2:1–4 NAB and NJB]).

   c. God will protect Jerusalem so that no wall is needed (Zech 2:1–5 [2:5–9 NAB and NJB]).

   d. The LORD promises Joshua the high priest that he will be in charge of the temple if he obeys the LORD; when the Branch (Zerubbabel) comes, God will forgive the land and give prosperity to everyone (Zech 3:1–10).

3. Examples of Revelation's use of images in Zechariah:
   - Seven golden lampstands (Zech 4:2; Rev 1:12)
   - Vision of a red horse and a white horse (Zech 1:8; Rev 6:2, 4)
   - A measuring line to measure Jerusalem (Zech 2:1–2 [2:5–6a NAB and NJB]) and the temple (Rev 11:1–2a)
   - Two olive trees and one/two lampstands (Zech 4:2–3, 11; Rev 11:4)

4. a. Points made by Leclerc about the Satan figure:
   - The figure of Satan is quite rare in the Old Testament, present in only three passages (Zech 3:1–12; Job 1–2; 1 Chr 21:1).
   - The Old Testament figure of Satan is not to be confused with the devil of later traditions.
   - Satan is not a personal name but more of a title.
   - Satan is the accuser, making charges against people and disclosing their wrongdoing before God.
   - The LORD is not always happy with the accusation of Satan, especially in Zechariah 3:1–2.

The prophetic experience is a sudden encounter with the meaning behind events.
— *John V. Taylor,* The Go-Between God

II.7 Isaiah 56–66

Assignment Objectives

To enable students to:

1. Describe some of the scholarly reasons for proposing the composite character of the Book of Isaiah and for identifying chapters 56–66 as Third Isaiah.
2. Identify the historical, social, and political events that provide the background for Isaiah 56–66.
3. Recognize the important themes of Third Isaiah, especially universal salvation, purification from sinfulness, and hopes for a new Zion.
4. Explain the possible overall organizational principles in the final editing of the Book of Isaiah.

Read

Isaiah 56–66; Leclerc, pages 360–75; "Restoration Literature: Overview—Third Isaiah," #9 in the SUPPLEMENTARY READINGS at the back of the student workbook

Rationale for Student Questions

To enable students:

1. To carefully read the text in order to determine the context and perspective of the biblical author.
2. To make connections between Third Isaiah and contemporary church and civic communities.
3. To reflect on the meaning of fasting as proclaimed by Third Isaiah.
4. To identify a prophetic text in its original context and its use in the liturgy today.
5. To identify a prophetic text in its original context and to see the text's relationship to the prophetic ministry of Jesus.
6. To read the prophetic text in a critical way in relation to its application today.

Suggested Lecture Topics

- Third Isaiah's relationship to the social, historical, and political events surrounding the return from exile.
- Composition of the Book of Isaiah, with an explanation of why most scholars divide the book into three separate sections from different time periods: Isaiah of Jerusalem, Second Isaiah, and Third Isaiah.
- Situations and theological themes for each division of the Book of Isaiah.
- Theological themes stressed in Third Isaiah, with discussion of how they are in continuity with the general tradition of Isaiah yet developed for the author's particular situation.
- Emphasis on proper fasting (Isa 58).
- Universal salvation.
- Holy Spirit.

SUGGESTED ANSWERS FOR UNIT II.7

1. Some passages that speak about ruin of the temple or surrounding area are:
   - Your ancient ruins shall be rebuilt for all generations (Isa 58:12; 61:4).
   - "Our adversaries have trampled down your sanctuary" (Isa 63:18).
   - "Jerusalem is desolation" (Isa 64:10).

3. a. Key points of the message about fasting are:
   - Fasting is not helping the people; they are serving only themselves (Isa 58:3).
   - Fasting that God desires is justice toward the downtrodden (Isa 58:6) and generosity to those who are hungry and naked (Isa 58:7); fasting in this way will bring God's response and reward (Isa 58:8–9).
   - Fasting is not acceptable to God when those who fast disregard God's ordinances and persist in their injustice (Isa 58:25).

5. b. Luke saw this passage of Isaiah fulfilled in the person of Jesus. Luke wants to show that Jesus inaugurated the messianic age proclaimed in Isaiah because Jesus had the same attitude toward the poor and oppressed as that expressed in these lines from Isaiah.

The prophet in Israel is not one who foretells but one who forthtells. *He speaks not with foresight into the future but with insight into the ways in which people have broken the covenant. The prophet is one who is called not only to speak on behalf of Yahweh, but one who speaks on behalf of those who have no voice.*

— John R. Donahue, SJ, "Biblical Perspectives on Justice,"
The Faith That Does Justice

II.8
Ezra 1:1–11, 3:1—10:17

Assignment Objectives

To enable students to:

1. Describe the person and mission of Ezra and his role in the spiritual and social restoration of the post-exilic Jewish community.
2. Recognize the important themes of the Book of Ezra, in particular the role of the Jewish law (Torah) in the renewal of Jewish life after the exile.

Read

Ezra 1:1–11, 3:1—10:17; Boadt, pages 453–55; EDB articles: "Beyond the River, #2," "Ezra, #1," "Jews, Judaism," "Persia," "Samaritans," and "Satrap"; "Restoration Literature: Overview—Ezra," #9 in the SUPPLEMENTARY READINGS at the back of the student workbook

Rationale for Student Questions

To enable students:

1. To recognize arguments both for and against the rebuilding of the temple and the city of Jerusalem.
2. To understand a biblical text in its own context and relate it to attitudes that might exist today.
3. To associate characteristics of a person with his leadership role.
4. To reflect on post-exilic attitudes that led to the dissolution of marriages with foreigners.
5. To recognize the ongoing importance of traditions within a religious community.

Suggested Lecture Topics

- Social and religious restoration after the exile.
- Chronology of events surrounding the career of Ezra and his work.
- Message of Ezra and the role he played in guiding the restoration community.
- Structure, composition, and characteristic theological themes of the Book of Ezra.

SUGGESTED ANSWERS FOR UNIT II.8

1. a. Cyrus authorized the rebuilding of temple (Ezra 5:13–17, 6:3–12).

   b. Arguments raised by adversaries against rebuilding:
      - Past rebellions of Jerusalem, perhaps a reference to Hezekiah, Josiah, and Zedekiah (Ezra 4:15).
      - Powerful kings from Jerusalem have dominated neighboring countries (Ezra 4:19–20).

3. Some things about Ezra that would help people respect him are:
   - He was a priest with a genealogy that could be traced to Zadok, David and Solomon's priest, and to Aaron (Ezra 7:1–5).
   - He was a scribe, learned in the Torah of Moses and observant of it (Ezra 7:6b).
   - He was backed by the authority and finances of the Persian King Artaxerxes (Ezra 7:6c).

Ezra's greatest contribution was to establish the Pentateuch as the authoritative canon for Jewish faith and practice. [As "canonical" or normative] the claim is made that this literature is sacred scripture and as such constitutes the community's rule for faith and conduct. In the time of Ezra and later, the authority of the Pentateuch was underscored by the dogma that this was none other than the "book of the Law of Moses" that had been delivered by God to Moses on Mount Sinai. Ezra probably introduced the Pentateuch as the officially recognized Mosaic tradition and, by his cultic reforms, brought Israel's life into conformity with this norm. He is rightly called "the father of Judaism," for under his influence the life and religion of the Jews were molded by the sacred Torah.

— Bernhard W. Anderson, Understanding the Old Testament

II.9 Nehemiah 1–2, 4–6 (3:33—6:19 NAB and NJB), 8–10, 13

Assignments Objectives

To enable students to:

1. Describe the person and work of Nehemiah in the historical and social context of the restoration of the Jewish community after the exile.
2. Recognize important themes in the Book of Nehemiah, especially Nehemiah's deep faith in God and his support of Torah and temple as the basis for administrative reforms for the restoration of the Jewish community.

Read

Nehemiah 1–2, 4–6 (3:33–6:19 NAB and NJB), 8–10, 13; Boadt, pages 455–60; EDB article: "Nehemiah, Book of"; "Restoration Literature: Overview—Nehemiah," #9 in the SUPPLEMENTARY READINGS at the back of the student workbook

Rationale for Student Questions

To enable students:

1. To describe the historical person of Nehemiah.
2. To recognize biblical models of prayer.
3. To investigate how Nehemiah solved post-exile problems and to relate those problems to situations today.
4. To analyze the text for possible connections between Ezra and the final redaction of the Torah.
5. To compare covenant renewal ceremonies from before and after the exile.
6. To explore the role of the laity in the contemporary world.

Suggested Lecture Topics

- Historical, social, and political situation that provides the background for the career of Nehemiah.
- Structure, composition, and particular theological themes expressed through the narrative of the Book of Nehemiah.
- Message of the Book of Nehemiah as it shapes the ideas and practices of the post-exilic Jewish community.
- Role of Ezra in covenant renewal and its placement in the Book of Nehemiah (8–10).

What page, what passage of the inspired books of the Old and New Testaments is not the truest of guides for human life?
— St. Benedict, Rule for Monasteries, 73.3

SUGGESTED ANSWERS FOR UNIT II.9

1. Nehemiah acted as a conscientious and capable governor when he:
   - personally inspected the wall (Neh 2:13b)
   - organized protection for the workers (Neh 4:9, 13–23 [4:3, 4–17 NAB and NJB])
   - assisted the people in rebuilding the walls of the city (Neh 5:16; implied in Neh 4:6 [3:38 NAB and NJB])
   - responded in anger to complaints of the Jewish people when they lost their land and held court against the nobles and officials (Neh 5:6–13)
   - refused to enrich himself at the expense of the people (Neh 5:14–15, 17–19)

2. a. We learn that Nehemiah prayed:
   - while in Persia, that God would forgive his people (Neh 1:4–11)
   - that he be sent to his people in Jerusalem (Neh 2:4)
   - because his people were being taunted by the leaders (Neh 4:4–5 [3:36–37 NAB and NJB])
   - to be remembered by God because of his generosity (Neh 5:19)
   - for his enemies (Neh 6:14)
   - that his good deeds might be remembered (Neh 13:14)
   - that God would favor and spare him (Neh 13:22b)
   - against the priests for defiling their priesthood and the covenant (Neh 13:29)

3. a. Some of the problems Nehemiah tried to remedy include:
   - The wall and gates were unprotected (Neh 1:3).
   - The poor were being oppressed by the rich (Neh 5:1–5).
   - Eliashib the priest had given Tobiah an apartment in the temple (Neh 13:4–5).
   - Levites had not been given their portions (Neh 13:10).
   - People were selling merchandise on the Sabbath (Neh 13:15–16).
   - Jews had married pagan women (Neh 13:23–24).

4. The fact that people came to the scribe Ezra "in order to study the words of the law" seems to imply that Ezra was extremely well-versed in these words (Neh 8:13). Second, Ezra was able to proclaim the people's history in great detail as if he had been involved in its editing (Neh 9:6–31). Finally, the text says that "we make a firm agreement in writing," which implies that Ezra was involved in sealing the final document (Neh 9:38, [10:1 NAB and NJB]).

5. Some elements unique to Ezra's covenant renewal are:
   - The people come fasting, in sackcloth, confessing their sins and those of their ancestors (Neh 9:1–2).
   - God is recognized as creator and the LORD alone (Neh 9:6).
   - The people "enter into a curse and an oath to walk in God's law" (Neh 10:29 [10:30 NAB and NJB]).
   - The people's agreement takes the form of a Sabbath observance and support of the temple (Neh 10:31–32 [10:32–33 NAB and NJB]).

II.10 Unit Two Review

Students will be responsible for:

1. A memory verse from one of the books that they studied during this unit, citing the reference and indicating the translation used.

2. The information included in the following SUPPLEMENTARY READINGS at the back of the student workbook:

   #8. "Literature of the Exile: Overview"

   #9. "Restoration Literature: Overview"

   #10. "Self-Quiz: Mid-Unit Two"

   #11. "Self-Quiz: Unit Two Map"

3. Demonstrating familiarity with the chronology of major events and people studied during this unit. They do not need to know dates, but must be able to place in chronological order the major events and characters. (For example, Second Isaiah comes *after* Ezekiel; Lamentations comes *before* Ezra.)

Suggested Lecture Topics

- Exilic and post-exilic books studied during this unit.
- Persons, places, events, themes, and terms connected with the Babylonian exile and the return and restoration of Judah.
- Geographical, social, and historical situations in which the prophets as well as Ezra and Nehemiah proclaimed God's word to the people.
- Chronology of major events and people studied during this year; give examples as in #3 above.
- Map exercises as above on map quiz.

YEAR THREE
UNIT TWO TEST

Name ______________________________

Center ________________ **Group #** _____

1. Match the following items with the appropriate book:

   Lamentations, Obadiah, Ezekiel, Second Isaiah, Haggai, Zechariah, Third Isaiah, Ezra, Nehemiah

   ____________ a. prophesied that the return from the exile was imminent

   ____________ b. human suffering from A–Z (acrostic)

   ____________ c. idols are impotent nothings

   ____________ d. mixed marriages broken up (give one of two possible answers)

   ____________ e. individual responsibility for one's own sins

   ____________ f. Israel is called Servant of the LORD

   ____________ g. book of consolation

   ____________ h. God's presence not limited to the temple; God was also present to the people in exile

   ____________ i. oracle against the Edomites

   ____________ j. rebuilding the walls of Jerusalem

   ____________ k. encouraged the rebuilding of the temple after the return from exile (give one of two possible answers)

   ____________ l. set in Jerusalem at the time of the fall of the city

   ____________ m. prophesied in Babylon at the beginning of the exile

   ____________ n. saw Cyrus as God's anointed

   ____________ o. saw people of all nations, even eunuchs, as welcome in the temple

   ____________ p. described a covenant renewal ceremony

   ____________ q. explored the theme of suffering as redemptive

   ____________ r. described Zion/Jerusalem as mother

   ____________ s. chastised the people for being concerned about their own homes/fields rather than rebuilding the temple

   ____________ t. post-exilic prophecy containing eight visions

   ____________ u. contains the Edict of Cyrus

2. a. What do you think is the most significant message of Second Isaiah?

b. How does this message apply to you today?

3. On the line before each prophet's name, indicate whether the prophet is pre-exilic, exilic, or post-exilic.

________	a. Jeremiah	________	f. Amos
________	b. Haggai	________	g. Third Isaiah
________	c. Zechariah	________	h. Ezekiel
________	d. Hosea	________	i. Isaiah of Jerusalem
________	e. Second Isaiah		

4. Describe the significance of Ezra and Nehemiah in forming the identity of the post-exilic community.

5. Chronology: In the blank between the columns, write whether the item in the first column came BEFORE or AFTER the item in the second column.

a. Ezekiel	________	Nehemiah
b. Ezra	________	Lamentations
c. Persian Empire	________	Babylonian Empire
d. Fall of the Northern Kingdom	________	Fall of the Southern Kingdom
e. Second Isaiah	________	Zechariah
f. Cyrus	________	Obadiah
g. Third Isaiah	________	Ezekiel

6. Write your memory verse from this unit, including reference and translation used.

7. What is the most significant thing you learned from this unit of study?

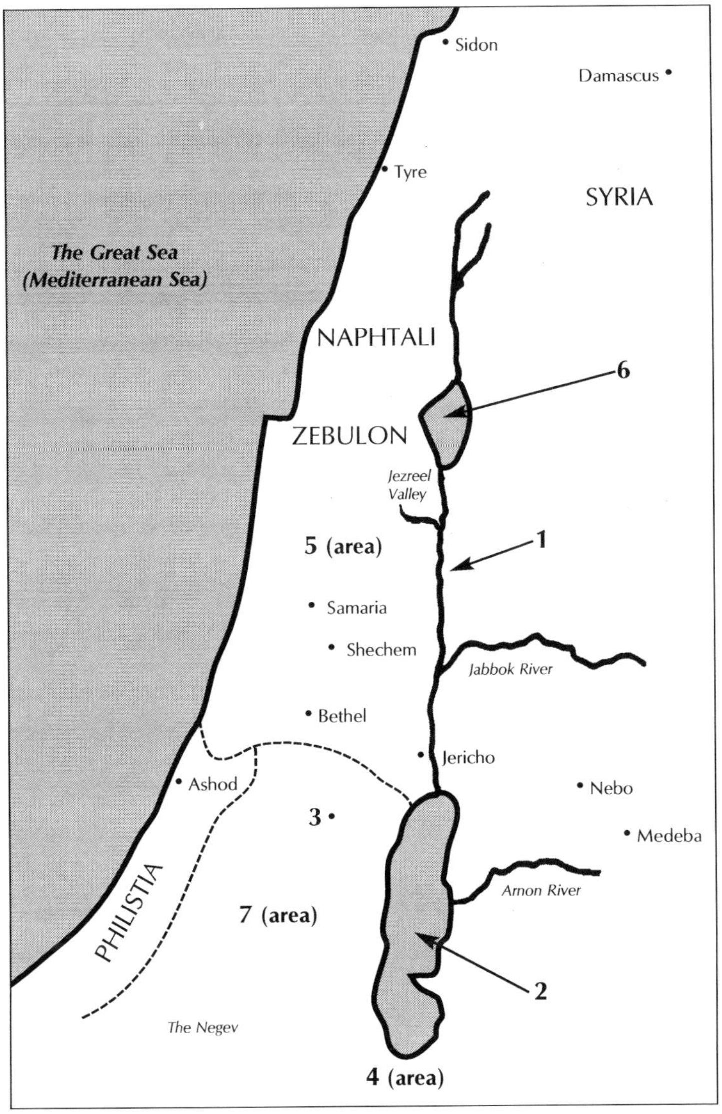

8. Map Test: In the blank next to each place name, write the number of the location on the map.

_____ a. Dead Sea

_____ b. Edom

_____ c. Jerusalem

_____ d. Judah

_____ e. Jordan River

_____ f. Samaria

_____ g. Sea of Galilee

ANSWERS TO YEAR THREE–UNIT TWO TEST

1. Matching Books with Themes

a. Second Isaiah
b. Lamentations
c. Second Isaiah
d. Ezra or Nehemiah
e. Ezekiel
f. Second Isaiah
g. Second Isaiah
h. Ezekiel
i. Obadiah
j. Nehemiah
k. Haggai or Zechariah
l. Lamentations
m. Ezekiel
n. Second Isaiah
o. Third Isaiah
p. Nehemiah
q. Second Isaiah
r. Third Isaiah
s. Haggai
t. Zechariah
u. Ezra

3. Time Periods of the Prophets

a. pre-exilic
b. post-exilic
c. post-exilic
d. pre-exilic
e. exilic
f. pre-exilic
g. post-exilic
h. exilic
i. pre-exilic

5. Chronology

a. Before
b. After
c. After
d. Before
e. Before
f. After
g. After

8. Map Test

a. 2
b. 4
c. 3
d. 7
e. 1
f. 5
g. 6

UNIT III
After the Exile

Objectives

To enable students to:

1. Describe the historical and social situation of post-exilic Israel.
2. Explain the message of the post-exilic prophets and its implications, especially for the New Testament.
3. Identify how the differing theological perspectives of the Chronicler and the Deuteronomistic Historian impact the writing of historical narratives, in particular by comparing 1 and 2 Chronicles with 1 and 2 Samuel and 1 and 2 Kings.
4. Discuss Hebrew poetry as exemplified in the Song of Solomon (Song of Songs) and the Book of Psalms.
5. Recognize the use of psalms in Christian prayer.

Textbooks

Primary Text: The Bible. Use a good translation with scholarly notes.

Other Texts: For helpful background and handy reference we recommend:

Eerdmans *Dictionary of the Bible* (cited as EDB)
Hammond's *Atlas of the Bible Lands* (cited as Hammond Atlas)
Lawrence Boadt's *Reading the Old Testament* (cited as Boadt)
Thomas L. Leclerc's *Introduction to the Prophets* (cited as Leclerc)

Assignments

Each lesson is to be studied by the students in preparation for their group discussion. For each biblical passage, students study the biblical text and footnotes for that particular passage, complete the other assigned readings, and do the written work *on a separate page*.

III.1 1 CHRONICLES 10–22, 28–29

III.2 2 CHRONICLES 1–9, 28–36

III.3 JOEL, MALACHI, ZECHARIAH 9–14

III.4 RUTH

III.5 SONG OF SOLOMON (SONG OF SONGS)

III.6 PSALMS I: HEBREW POETRY AND ITS USE IN CHRISTIAN LITURGY (Psalms 1, 15, 22, 34, 51, 104, 119, 141)

III.7 PSALMS II: SUPPLICATION AND LAMENT (Psalms 3, 5, 6, 14, 32, 38, 74, 80, 88, 109, 130, 137, 139:19–22)

III.8 PSALMS III: CONFIDENCE, THANKSGIVING, AND PRAISE (Psalms 2, 8, 23, 27, 29, 30, 33, 45, 48, 62, 65, 72, 91, 92, 100, 101, 110, 113, 116, 118, 124, 131, 132, 148, 150)

III.9 PSALMS IV: REVIEWING THE STORY OF ISRAEL (Psalms 37, 47, 49, 50, 78, 82, 89, 95, 96, 105, 106, 135, 136)

III.10 UNIT THREE REVIEW

UNIT THREE TEST

III.1
1 Chronicles 10–22, 28–29

Assignment Objectives

To enable students to:

1. Identify the religious, social, political, and historical situation of the post-exilic Jewish community for which the Books of Chronicles were written.
2. Recognize the Chronicler's reinterpretation of the history of Israel as a covenant relationship that demanded an obedient response to the Mosaic Law.
3. Explain the Chronicler's redaction of his sources, in particular the Deuteronomistic History of Israel.
4. Better understand the expectations of ancient Jewish readers regarding history and the different ways in which history was written.

Read

1 Chronicles 10–22, 28–29; Boadt, pages 449–53; EDB article: "Historiography, Biblical: Biblical Historical Writing"; "David, the King: Two Biblical Portraits," #12, "Synoptic Comparison 1: The Bringing of the Ark to Jerusalem," #13, and "After the Exile: Overview—The Chronicler's History," #14 in the SUPPLEMENTARY READINGS at the back of the student workbook

Rationale for Student Questions

To enable students:

1. To reflect on the author's redaction of sources in order to see how the text has been fashioned for post-exilic readers.

2, 3. To recognize how the author shaped his sources to express his own message.

4. To note how two different accounts are shaped to express each author's message.
5. To recognize the author's portrait of David as a model for the readers in their historical and social situation.
6. To apply the biblical text to their own lives.

Suggested Lecture Topics

- Social, political, and historical situation of the Jewish post-exilic community.
- Theological and social problems faced by the post-exilic Jews as they tried to restore their community.
- Rewriting of history as a way of addressing the problems faced by the post-exilic community.
- Connections between the Deuteronomistic History found in the Books of Samuel and Kings and the work of the Chronicler.
- Motives for composition, structure, strategies, redactional techniques, and theological themes that characterize the Chronicler's history.
- Typology (i.e., using persons or patterns of behavior as the representation and embodiment of values that the author holds and wishes to persuade the readers to adopt).
- Historical writing in ancient times, in particular how the expectations were different from our expectations.
- David as the traditional author of some of the psalms based on 1 Chronicles 16.
- Role of the Levites in the post-exilic community.

SUGGESTED ANSWERS FOR UNIT III.1

1. a. Ways in which the Chronicler edits 2 Samuel 6:
    - David claims that the ark was neglected in the time of Saul (1 Chr 13:1–4).
    - 1 Chronicles 14:1—15:24 is an addition.
    - Chronicles says that the Levites carried the ark, as Moses had prescribed (1 Chr 15:2, 15, 26) and had special responsibilities (1 Chr 16:4–7).
    - Chronicles softens David's rebuke of Michal (2 Sam 6:20–23 has no parallel).

   b. In the Chronicler's time, the priests and the Levites were distinct groups. The Chronicler gives more prominence to the Levites vis-à-vis the priests. He provides theological justification for the role that the levitical priests had assumed by the time of the book's writing.

2. a. 1 Chronicles 16:8–36 is a compilation of the following psalms:
   Psalm 105:1–15 (1 Chr 16:8–22)
   Psalm 96:1–13 (1 Chr 16:23–33)
   Psalm 106:1, 47–48 (1 Chr 16:34–36)

   b. These psalms were most likely chosen because they are psalms of praise.

   c. The Chronicler portrays these psalms as being sung by levitical priests in the time of David. In so doing, the Chronicler is saying that the psalms have their roots in the time of David.

3. a. i. In 1 Chronicles 20, the Chronicler omits the painful truth of David's sin with Bathsheba and all its consequences.
   ii. Certainly passing over this incident in silence does not erase it from the people's memory, but it does draw attention to David as a model of upright conduct.

   b. i. In 1 Chronicles 21 the Chronicler has added a context for the taking of the census by integrating it into the story of the building of the temple. He also has added the Satan figure who is instrumental in enticing David to sin.
   ii. God's anger is not the motivating factor. The sin lies in David. Thus, David must bear the full responsibility for the sin.

4. a. The entire story of David's deterioration, the struggle among his sons for the throne, and the influence of Bathsheba in David's choice of Solomon are omitted by the Chromicler. In 1 Kings, David bequeaths political power to Solomon and gives instructions about settling old political scores. The temple is not mentioned. In 1 Chronicles, the handing over of the kingship is identified with David's commissioning of Solomon to build the temple and providing him with materials and detailed instructions for doing so.

   b. Solomon's role in designing the temple is minimized (1 Chr 28:11–21). Solomon's reign is portrayed as glorious (1 Chr 29:23–25) and exalted. He is chosen solely by God to be king (1 Chr 29:1).

5. David is often portrayed at prayer. The temple is central. The Chronicler tells the story in this way to impress upon his post-exilic community the centrality of prayer and the temple in living out their lives as people of God.

III.2
2 Chronicles 1–9, 28–36

Assignment Objectives

To enable students to:

1. Describe more fully the situation, message, and theology of the Chronicler's history and its role in post-exilic Judaism.
2. Recognize the major themes of the Chronicler's history, in particular the centrality of the temple for the restored people of Judah.
3. Analyze the way in which the post-exilic Jews used history to further their goals of restoration.

Read

2 Chronicles 1–9, 28–36; EDB article: "Levites"; "After the Exile: Overview—The Chronicler's History," #14, "Synoptic Comparison 2: Solomon's Prayer," #15, and "Prayer of Manasseh," #16 in the SUPPLEMENTARY READINGS at the back of the student workbook

Rationale for Student Questions

To enable students:

1. To reflect on the author's redaction of his sources.
2. To note a basic theological theme of the author.
3. To recognize the centrality of the temple in the post-exilic community and to point out the Chronicler's reinterpretation of history.
4. To recognize the reinterpretation of history as a means of shaping a theological message.
5. To appropriate the insights from this lesson by learning to recognize instances of reinterpretation in their own experience.

Suggested Lecture Topics

- Structure, composition, strategy, and theological themes that characterize 2 Chronicles in relation to the social, political, and historical situation after the exile.
- Symbolic meaning of the temple and its significance for the post-exilic Jewish community.
- Ancient authors' creative use of sources to write historical narrative.
- Immediate retribution.
- Why new situations might require a reinterpretation of history.
- Prayer of Manasseh.

SUGGESTED ANSWERS FOR UNIT III.2

1. a. The Chronicler has added the following details:
    - Fire from heaven consumed the sacrifice (2 Chr 7:1).
    - The glory of the LORD filled the house, preventing the priests from entering it (2 Chr 7:2).
    - When the people saw this, they bowed down, worshiped, and gave thanks to the LORD (2 Chr 7:3).
    - The Chronicler has also deleted Solomon's speech (1 Kgs 8:56–61).

2. The LORD will be faithful to the covenant he made with David if the people uphold their end of the covenant. They must humble themselves, pray, seek God's face, and turn from their wicked ways. They must not worship foreign gods. They must not forsake the commands of the LORD.

3. a. The Chronicler has added the following:
    - Solomon gave instructions to the priests and Levites, listing them by name as the ones that the LORD had chosen (2 Chr 29:12–14). 2 Kings makes no mention of the fact that they cleansed the house of the LORD.
    - Hezekiah led the people in offering holocausts and sacrifice.
    - Priests and Levites assisted in various ways (2 Chr 29:20–36).
    - Hezekiah invited all Israel to participate in the Passover, but many spurned the invitation.
    - Judah was of one mind in carrying out the order of the king (2 Chr 30).
    - Hezekiah reestablished the classes of priests and Levites (2 Chr 31:2).
    - Hezekiah instituted a tithe that was to be used for the priests and Levites, which the people supported so generously that special houses had to be constructed for the abundance (2 Chr 31:4–11).
    - Priests and Levites were assigned special duties and given authority over certain cities (2 Chr 31:12–19).

4. a. Manasseh had one of the longest reigns of any king in Judah. The Chronicler wants to explain theologically how he could have had this long reign when in fact he was one of the worst kings (2 Chr 33:1–9) and led the people to do abominable things.

The Chronicler's contribution is to show the meaning of the past to contemporary situations. It is here that we see the Chronicler "preaching" his people's history. His themes of preaching are consistent and limited, but they are profound. It has often been supposed that he presents merely a rather rigid view of divine retribution, and applies this doctrine blindly to his material. What seems much clearer is that he sees a great overall pattern in experience, and that this is presented in terms of failure and judgment, grace and restoration... He sees his contemporaries in the middle of the great new era of restoration, though he is fully aware of the problems which being a subject people presents for the recognition of that ideal. He traces through the earlier history a pattern of unbelief and disaster, of faith and restoration, which provides a theological unity for the whole.

— *Peter Ackroyd,* I and II Chronicles, Ezra, Nehemiah

III.3
Joel, Malachi, Zechariah 9–14

Assignment Objectives

To enable students to:

1. Identify the social, political, and historical situations that provoked the prophetic oracles of Joel, Malachi, and Deutero-Zechariah.
2. Recognize the structure, message, prophetic styles, and theological themes that characterize the prophecies of Joel, Malachi, and Deutero-Zechariah.
3. Note how the New Testament writers used passages from Joel, Malachi, and Deutero-Zechariah to clarify their understanding of New Testament events.

Read

Joel, Malachi, Zechariah 9–14; Leclerc, pages 346–59 and 375–82; EDB article: "Locust"; "After the Exile: Overview—Joel, Malachi, and Deutero-Zechariah," #14 in the SUPPLEMENTARY READINGS at the back of the student workbook

Rationale for Student Questions

To enable students:

1. To reflect upon Luke's use of Joel and to note why the prophet Joel might have appealed to Luke.
2. To recognize the changes in the prophetic tradition due to the changing contexts.
3. To notice the prophet's identification of sin and appeal to the prophetic tradition of using the marriage analogy.
4. To reflect upon Matthew's use of Malachi and to recognize why the prophet Malachi might have appealed to Matthew.
5. To reinforce understanding of the prophetic style of Malachi.
6. To reflect on Matthew's and John's use of Deutero-Zechariah and to recognize why the prophet Deutero-Zechariah might have appealed to these evangelists.

Suggested Lecture Topics

- Social, political, and historical events that provide the background for the messages of Joel, Malachi, and Deutero-Zechariah.
- Structure, composition, literary images, and theological themes that characterize Joel, Malachi, and Deutero-Zechariah.
- Prophetic theology's use of ordinary events to gain insight into the extraordinary workings of God.
- Structure of the teaching dialogue as used by Malachi.
- Relationship between Zechariah 9–14 and Zechariah 1–8.
- Connections between post-exilic prophecy and apocalyptic literature.
- Use of Old Testament prophets by New Testament authors.

SUGGESTED ANSWERS FOR UNIT III.3

1. Luke uses a text from Joel to connect the main themes of his theology in Acts of the Apostles (see Acts 1:6–9): the Holy Spirit comes down on the disciples (church) as the impetus to their prophetic ministry of witness in word and deed, signaling the coming of God for the salvation of all humanity.

3. a. Divorce, intermarriage with foreigners

   b. For Malachi, the fact that the men of Judah were divorcing their Jewish wives to marry foreigners was a violation of the covenant (Mal 2:10).

4. a. i. Matthew portrays John the Baptist as a prophet in the manner of Elijah.
      ii. Matthew identifies John as the messenger (Matt 11:10; Mal 3:1) and as the Elijah to come (Matt 11:14; Mal 4:5 [3:23 NAB and NJB]).
      iii. After the transfiguration, Matthew has Jesus answer the question of the disciples about Elijah's coming by saying that Elijah has already come.

   b. John the Baptist is identified as the messenger and as the returning Elijah. Since the promised messiah comes after the messenger, Jesus must be the messiah. If Elijah has come, then the new age has begun.

6. a. i. The king will enter not like a warrior (riding a horse) but in meekness, riding a colt, the foal of a donkey. Symbolically, this means that the king will bring peace, not war.
      ii. Matthew interprets these verses literally, to the point that Jesus rides two animals!

   b. i. The original context of this verse may refer to King Josiah, but most probably it refers to an unnamed sufferer much like the Suffering Servant of Second Isaiah.
      ii. The Gospel of John sees the verse fulfilled literally when the soldier thrusts a lance through the side of Jesus' corpse.

I am convinced that for a Christian today in this complex, difficult and secularized Western society it is practically impossible to persevere in the faith without drawing sustenance, even on one's own, from Scripture.

– Cardinal Carlo Martini, "Teaching the Scriptures to a Diocese,"
Priests and People, June, 1992

III.4 Ruth

Assignment Objectives

To enable students to:

1. Describe the literary form of the Book of Ruth as a short story about an ancestor of David.
2. Recognize how the author employs plot, character, setting, and themes.
3. Identify specific themes of the Book of Ruth, especially divine providence, covenant fidelity, and openness to foreigners.

Read

Ruth; Boadt, pages 500–01; EDB articles: "Gleaning," "Levirate Marriage," and "Ruth, Book of"; "After the Exile: Overview—Ruth," #14 in the SUPPLEMENTARY READINGS at the back of the student workbook

Rationale for Student Questions

To enable students:

1. To recall the legal background for the events depicted in the story of Ruth and thus to understand better the historical, social, and religious situation of the times.
2. To recognize the author's use of God as an "off-stage character."
3. To develop skills in building a character portrait from the text.
4. To explore the possible meaning of the story and what the author may have intended for the original audience.
5. To draw associations between the experiences of Ruth as depicted in the text and experiences that they themselves or people they know have had.

Suggested Lecture Topics

- Possible dating—pre-exilic or post-exilic—for the Book of Ruth.
- Literary genre, structure, and the basic themes of Ruth.
- Literary genre of a biblical book as the key to its interpretation.
- Review of *Dei Verbum* §10, §11, and §12 found in the Second Year Student Workbook, SUPPLEMENTARY READING #1, "Truth and Its Many Expressions."
- Biblical books as not necessarily historical:
  - A fictionalized short story as a medium for divine revelation.
  - A didactic short story as a popular genre of literature in post-exilic Judaism.
  - Role of fictional short story in teaching.
  - Message of a fictional short story as conveyed by the use of plot, character, setting, and themes.

SUGGESTED ANSWERS FOR UNIT III.4

1. a. Deuteronomy 24:19–22; 25:5–10; Genesis 38; Leviticus 19:9–10; 23:22.

2. a. The LORD is not so much a central character in the Book of Ruth as an "off-stage" character to whom reference is made (Ruth 1:6, 16, 21; 2:4, 12; 3:10, 13; 4:11–14).

4. The book is positive in its description of Ruth, the foreigner. Unlike the Books of Ezra (9–10), Nehemiah (9:2; 13:23–31), and Malachi (2:11) that strongly denounce marriages outside of the Jewish community, the Book of Ruth accepts and approves of Ruth's marriage to Boaz (Ruth 1:4, 18, 22; 2:11–13; 3:1, 11; 4:5, 10–13).

Indeed the authority of Scripture seemed to be more to be revered and more worthy of devoted faith in that it was at once a book that all could read and read easily, and yet preserved the majesty of its mystery in the deepest part of its meaning: for it offers itself to all in the plainest words and the simplest expressions, yet demands the closest attention of the most serious minds.

— *Augustine,* Confessions, *6:5*

III.5 Song of Solomon (Song of Songs)

Assignment Objectives

To enable students to:

1. Identify the Song of Solomon (Song of Songs) as Hebrew poetry by examining its structure, images, and symbols.
2. Recognize the connection between human and divine love as illustrated through the collection of love lyrics in the Song of Solomon (Song of Songs).
3. Explain possible allegorical interpretations of the Song of Solomon (Song of Songs).

Read

Song of Solomon (Song of Songs); Boadt, pages 485–86; EDB articles: "Allegory," "Poetry," and "Song of Solomon"; "After the Exile: Overview—Song of Solomon (Song of Songs)," #14 in the SUPPLEMENTARY READINGS at the back of the student workbook

Rationale for Student Questions

To enable students:

1. To make connections with other biblical books regarding the theme of spousal love.
2. To develop skill in recognizing and understanding both the literal and the spiritual dimensions of the text.
3. To trace imagery through the book and to see how the poet is employing images to evoke a response.
4. To recognize that the descriptions of beauty used by the author may differ from current descriptions and to express the message using modern forms.
5. To recognize that the poem has meaning as a whole and to articulate that meaning.

Suggested Lecture Topics

- Attribution of authorship to Solomon.
- Basics of poetic expression, in particular the evocation of strong feelings like love.
- Parallelism as the distinctive characteristic of poetic expression for Hebrew poetry.
- Literary genre, approximate date, structure, imagery, and themes that characterize the Song of Solomon (Song of Songs).
- No overt mention of God.
- Canonical book despite the subject matter and suggestive imagery.
- Interpreting these songs as:
  - having to do with human love.
  - an allegory of the love between God and Israel.
  - an allegory of the love between Christ and the church.
  - an allegory of the love between God and the individual soul (e.g., St. Bernard).

SUGGESTED ANSWERS FOR UNIT III.5

1. There are many places in the Bible where God's love for Israel is described in terms of love between a man and a woman. These instances include:
   - God says that Israel will refer to him as "my husband" and not "my master (or my baal)" (Hos 1–3, especially 2:18–22).
   - Israel is seen as a wife whom the Lord has called back (Isa 54:4–8).
   - God will rejoice in Israel as a bridegroom rejoices in his bride (Isa 62:4–5).
   - Israel loved God as a bride (Jer 2:2).
   - The infidelity of Israel to God is compared to the infidelity of a woman to her lover (Jer 3:20).
   - Israel's coming to maturity and breaking faith is seen in terms of a woman reaching puberty and playing the harlot (Ezek 16).
   - The story is told of God and two sisters, each of whom spurns God's love and plays the harlot with others (Ezek 23).
   - The relationship between Christ and the church is seen in marital terms in that Christ gives himself for the church (Eph 5:25–33).
   - Reference is made to the wedding feast of the lamb of God (Rev 19:7–9).
   - The wife of the lamb is the new city of Jerusalem (Rev 21:2, 9–14).

Israel resisted the divinization of sexuality characteristic of the ancient Near-East. The Lord had no female consort. Human sexual love was seen as intrinsically good; it could even be a symbol of divine love. [The Song of Songs] presents us with a biblical model of human intimacy. The mutuality and fidelity between lovers, the sensuousness of their relationship, their devotion to each other, clearly emerge... It is widely held that the sages of Israel are responsible for its preservation and transmission because they recognized a sound expression of the values of human love. Christianity can be grateful for this insight.

Roland E. Murphy, O Carm, "Canticle of Canticles,"
The New Jerome Biblical Commentary

III.6
Psalms I: Hebrew Poetry and Its Use in Christian Liturgy

Assignment Objectives

To enable students to:

1. Describe the diversity of genres in the Book of Psalms.
2. Explain some of the structural features of Hebrew poetry, in particular the use of parallelism and alphabetic construction.
3. Recognize how the images and themes of the psalms were used by Christians to illuminate their understanding of God and Jesus.
4. Explain the use of the psalms in Christian prayer.

Read

Psalms 1, 15, 22, 34, 51, 104, 119, 141; Boadt, pages 279–90; "After the Exile: Overview—Psalms," #14 in the SUPPLEMENTARY READINGS at the back of the student workbook

Rationale for Student Questions

To enable students:

1. To identify parallel construction in Hebrew poetry and to reflect on its use and effectiveness in conveying the author's message.
2. To recognize the common cosmography expressed by certain psalms and Genesis.
3. To respond to the content of a psalm.
4. To reflect upon the use of Psalm 22 by Christian authors to illuminate the meaning of the death of Jesus.
5. To recognize the importance and the meaning of the law for the ancient Israelites.
6. To apply the insights of the psalms to modern occasions.

Suggested Lecture Topics

- Structure of the Book of Psalms and the historical process of its collection.
- Structural features of Hebrew poetry, in particular the use of parallelism.
- Hebrew poetry within the broader context of ancient Near Eastern poetry.
- Diversity of materials found in the collection of psalms.
- Authorship of the psalms attributed to David.
- Purpose of the psalms and their relationship to specific situations.
- Use of psalms in Jewish prayer and the community's familiarity with their form and content.
- Use of psalms in Christian prayer, particularly in the eucharistic liturgy and the Liturgy of the Hours.
- Use of psalms in a Christological sense.
- Law as something good, not as a "burden" or "yoke."

SUGGESTED ANSWERS FOR UNIT III.6

1. Psalm 1:6 (A); Psalm 15:1 (S); Psalm 22:12 (22:13 NAB) (S); Psalm 34:10 (34:11 NAB) (A); Psalm 34:13 (34:14 NAB) (S); Psalm 34:19 (34:20 NAB) (O); Psalm 51:7 (51:9 NAB) (S); Psalm 51:13 (51:15 NAB) (O); Psalm 104:28 (S); Psalm 119:72 (O); Psalm 119:105 (S); Psalm 141:3 (S).

2. Similar views of the created world expressed by Psalm 104 and Genesis 1 may include:
   - The heavens are spread out like a tent (Ps 104:1; Gen 1:6–8).
   - The ocean covered the earth, but never again (Ps 104:6–9; Gen 1:9; see also Gen 6–9).
   - The moon and sun mark the seasons (Psalm 104:19; Gen 1:14).

5. a. The law is referred to as (these are repeated throughout the psalm):
   - God's decrees/instructions (Ps 119:2)
   - God's ways (Ps 119:3)
   - Precepts (Ps 119:4)
   - Statutes (Ps 119:5)
   - Commandments/commands (Ps 119:6)
   - Ordinances/edicts/judgments (Ps 119:7)
   - Word/promise (Ps 119:11)

5. b. The psalmist has a positive attitude toward God's law, which is a cause of joy in itself. Though the psalmist may suffer for doing what is right, he hopes and prays that God will vindicate him and punish the evildoers, for God's own sake.

The Psalms' chief formal characteristic, the most obvious element of pattern, is fortunately one that survives in translation. Most readers will know that I mean what scholars call "parallelism"... It is either a wonderful piece of luck or a wise provision of God's, that poetry which was to be turned into all languages should have as its chief formal characteristic one that does not disappear in translation.

— *C. S. Lewis,* Reflections on the Psalms

III.7
Psalms II: Supplication and Lament

Assignment Objectives

To enable students to:

1. Describe the structure and characteristic themes of the lament form as used in Hebrew poetry.
2. Recognize the lament psalms and reflect on their function in the liturgical and social life of ancient Israel.
3. Recognize the application and use of the lament psalms for their own prayer.
4. Identify distinctive literary forms of the psalms.

Read

Psalms 3, 5, 6, 88 (individual laments); Psalms 14, 74, 80, 137 (communal laments); Psalms 32, 38, 130 (penitential psalms); Psalms 109, 139:19–22 (cursing psalms); EDB articles: "Curse," "Lament," and "Sheol"; "Types of Psalms," #18 in the SUPPLEMENTARY READINGS at the back of the student workbook

Rationale for Student Questions

To enable students:

1. To recognize the element of petition in the structure of the lament and to identify some of the various reasons advanced by the poet for trust in God.
2. To reflect on the question of the Hebrew belief in an afterlife, a belief that developed over time and was not always clear.
3. To interact with the lament genre in a more active way by writing a lament.
4. To recognize the lament form in the prophet Jeremiah and refresh the students' memory of Jeremiah's experience.
5. To reflect on a problem area that might arise when reading or praying certain psalms.

Suggested Lecture Topics

- Structural components of the lament form, especially the pattern that often ends on an upbeat note of faith or trust in God.
- Lament form connected to the situations that normally invite its use both for personal and communal prayer.
- Presence of the lament form outside the Book of Psalms (e.g., in the Book of Lamentations and the prophets that were studied in previous units).
- Appropriate situations for the use of lament psalms today.

SUGGESTED ANSWER FOR UNIT III.7

2. The psalmist does not seem to recognize a "meaningful afterlife" for he laments, "in death there is no remembrance of you; in Sheol who can give you praise?" (Ps 6:5).

The psalms are an assurance to us that when we pray and worship, we are not expected to censure or deny the deepness of our own human pilgrimage. Rather, we are expected to submit it openly and trustingly so that it can be brought to eloquent and passionate speech addressed to the Holy One... The psalms move with our experience. They may also take us beyond our own guarded experience, into the more poignant pilgrimage of our sisters and brothers.

— *Walter Brueggemann,* Praying with the Psalms

III.8
Psalms III: Confidence, Thanksgiving, and Praise

Assignment Objectives

To enable students to:

1. Identify the structure, characteristic themes, and situations that give rise to the psalms of confidence, thanksgiving, and praise.
2. Recognize the royal psalms and reflect on their function in the liturgical and social life of ancient Israel.
3. Appreciate the theological diversity and the emotional variety expressed in the psalms.
4. Consider how the psalms of confidence, thanksgiving, and praise might be used in their own prayer.

Read

Psalm 23 and *one* of the following: 27, 62, 91, 131 (psalms of confidence/trust); *one* of the following: psalms 30, 92, 116 (psalms of individual thanksgiving); Psalm 118 and *one* of the following: 65, 124 (psalms of communal thanksgiving); Psalms 8, 29, 33, 48, 100 and *one* of the following: 113, 148, 150 (psalms of praise); Psalm 110 and *one* of the following: 2, 45, 72, 101, 132 (royal psalms)

Rationale for Student Questions

To enable students:

1. To recognize the variety of reasons for praising God.
2. To recognize the historical setting of a royal enthronement psalm and how it was used later by Christians.
3. To explain the historical setting of one particular psalm.
4. To explore the reasoning of the psalmist.
5. To connect the psalmist's insight into God's fidelity with their own experience.
6. To compose prayers in the style of the psalms.

Suggested Lecture Topics

- Structural components of the psalms of confidence, thanksgiving, and praise.
- Trust as a key to the psalmist's understanding of God.
- Situations that normally invite the use of psalms of confidence, thanksgiving, and praise for both personal and communal prayer.
- Disposition of thanks and praise that permeates Old Testament theology and life and spills over into the Christian eucharistic attitude.
- Characteristics of royal psalms and their place in the social and liturgical life of the ancient Israelites.
- Old Testament theology reflected in the psalms.

SUGGESTED ANSWERS FOR UNIT III.8

1. We are invited to praise God for:
    - The LORD's name (Ps 8:1, 9 [8:2, 10 NAB])
    - The creation of humanity as little less than the gods (Ps 8:4–8 [8:5–9 NAB])
    - God's power and majesty described in the imagery of a violent thunderstorm (Ps 29:3–9) and for the power of God's word ("voice of the LORD" is used seven times in Ps 29)
    - The creative power of God manifested in God's word (Ps 33:4–9) and God's providence and care for Israel (Ps 33:10–19)
    - The deliverance of Jerusalem (Zion) from destruction (Ps 48)
    - Making Israel God's people (Ps 100:3)
    - God's faithfulness and steadfast love (Hebrew *hesed*) to all generations (Ps 100:5)

2. a. In its original context, Psalm 110 was a royal enthronement psalm (i.e., it was sung on the occasion of a new king being seated on the throne).

    b. Jesus' being seated at the right hand of God was understood to have happened after his death. It is another way of expressing the same fundamental faith statement of Jesus' being raised from the dead. Psalm 110 was quoted by New Testament authors many times (e.g., Ps 110:1 is used in Matt 22:44; Mark 12:36; Luke 20:42–43; Acts 2:34; and Heb 1:13; 10:12–13); Psalm 110:4 is used in Hebrews 5:6 and 7:17. There are also many allusions to this psalm elsewhere in the New Testament.

3. Some indications that Psalm 118 was used in the temple are the antiphonal nature of these verses (Ps 118:1–4) and the following statements:
    - "Let the house of Aaron say…" (Ps 118:3).
    - "Open to me the gates of righteousness, that I may enter through them and give thanks to the LORD" (Ps 118:19).
    - "This is the gate of the LORD; the righteous shall enter through it" (Ps 118:20).
    - "Blessed is the one who comes in the name of the LORD" (Ps 118:26a).
    - "We bless you from the house of the LORD" (Ps 118:26b).
    - "Bind the festal procession with branches, up to the horns of the altar" (Ps 118:27b).
    - "You are my God, and I give thanks to you" (Ps 118:28).
    - "O give thanks to the LORD, for he is good" (Ps 118:29).

5. Some characteristics of God that form the basis of our trust:
    - God is faithful (Ps 23:4; Ps 27:5).
    - God is powerful (Ps 62:11 [62:12 NAB]).
    - God is our protector (Ps 23:4; Ps 27:1–3, 5; Ps 62:1–2 [62:2–3 NAB], 6 [7 NAB]; Ps 91:2–13).
    - God loves and cares for us (Ps 23:1–4; Ps 91:15; Ps 131:2).
    - God is merciful and compassionate (Ps 27:10).
    - God is generous (Ps 23:5).
    - God is good (Ps 17:13).

III.9 Psalms IV: Reviewing the Story of Israel

Assignment Objectives

To enable students to:

1. Recognize the use of psalms to recount and illuminate the major events of Israelite history.
2. Note how the psalms express a theology of God in relation to the world and the people of Israel.
3. Appreciate how the psalms express the feelings and moods that we have in our relationship with God.

Read

Psalms 78, 105, 106, 135, 136 (narratives/historical psalms); Psalms 50, 82 (prophetic psalms); Psalms 37, 49 (wisdom psalms); Psalms 47, 95, 96 (The LORD is King); Psalm 89 (messianic psalm); "Rereadings (Relectures)," #19 in the SUPPLEMENTARY READINGS at the back of the student workbook

Rationale for Student Questions

To enable students:

1. To review the psalmists' understanding of the Mosaic covenant as important in the life of the people of Israel.
2. To review the psalmist's understanding of the Davidic covenant promises and their importance in the life of the people of Israel.
3. To review the Old Testament theme of retribution (as exemplified also in the Book of Deuteronomy and the prophets) and to reflect on how and why our Christian understanding might be different.
4. To review the theme of God's divine sovereignty, in particular through the imagery of God as king, and to reflect on what it might mean today.
5. To reflect on the psalmists' approach to conversion and to connect it to that of a prophet previously studied.

Suggested Lecture Topics

- Background, characteristics, structure, themes, and situations of the narrative/historical, prophetic, wisdom, and messianic psalms.
- Psalms that incorporate and express the most important events in the history of the ancient Israelites.
- Review of Israel's history, noting the major dates and making connections with both first-year and previous third-year material.
- Major themes that appear in the questions (i.e., the Mosaic covenant, the Davidic covenant, retribution and judgment, conversion, God alone as supreme).

If the Psalm prays, do you too pray, if it laments, so do you too, if it renders thanks, so do you also rejoice with it; if it hopes, so you too; if it speaks in the accents of fear, do you also tremble with it; for all that is written therein is meant to be a mirror for us.

— *St. Augustine,* Sermons on the Psalms, *30*

SUGGESTED ANSWERS FOR UNIT III.9

1. Possible answers might be:
    - God is creator; all we have is from God (Ps 136:4–9).
    - God alone is God, greater than any idol we might set up for ourselves (Ps 135:5, 15–18).
    - We have been chosen as God's people (Ps 135:4).
    - God has done marvelous things for us in the past and will continue to be faithful in the future (Ps 135:8–14; Ps 136:4, 10–22).

2. a. The following promises are made:
    - God will always be with them (Ps 89: 21, 24, 28 [89:22, 25, 29 NAB]).
    - The Davidic line will endure (Ps 89:4, 29, 34–36 [89:5, 30, 35–37 NAB]).
    - God will be David's support and strength (Ps 89:21–24 [89:22–25 NAB]).
    - David is brought into special relationship with God (Ps 89:26–27 [89:27–28 NAB]).

    b. If David's descendants violate God's laws, they will be punished; but the punishment will not last forever. God will not violate the covenant (Ps 89:30–34 [89:31–35 NAB]).

    c. Psalm 89:38–48 (89:39–49 NAB) was likely added to the psalm as a result of the exile, for the section begins with "but now." Moreover, the psalmist is describing a situation where Jerusalem has been destroyed and the anointed one has been defeated. The anger of the LORD is still smoldering, thus reflecting the likelihood that the exiles have not yet returned to the land.

3. a. The psalmist states that even though present appearances indicate that the wicked prosper and the good suffer, God will in time reward the good (symbolized by ownership of the land) and punish the wicked here on earth. One needs only to wait for the LORD to act (Ps 37:7, 34).

4. a. God is identified as king because:
    - God conquers the enemies of Israel (Ps 47:3 [47:4 NAB]) and has given Israel the land of Canaan (Ps 47:4 [47:5 NAB]); God reigns over all nations (Ps 47:7–8 [47:8–9 NAB]).
    - God is savior (Ps 95:1); God has created everything (Ps 95:4–5); God protects and cares for the covenanted people of Israel (Ps 95:7).
    - God is creator (Ps 96:5b) and judge (Ps 96:10, 13).

    b. Some appropriate responses might be:
    - Praise, song, and exultation (Ps 47:1 [47:2 NAB], 5–6 [6–7 NAB]; Ps 95:2; Ps 96:1)
    - Worship (Ps 95:2, 6)
    - Following God's ways (Ps 95:8–10)
    - Making God's glory known throughout the world (Ps 96:3)

5. a. Like many of the prophets, the psalmist warns against religious formalism (going through the external religious rituals but not living one's life according to God's ways). Proper worship must be accompanied by righteous living (i.e., fidelity to the covenant and justice to the poor and oppressed).

III.10
Unit Three Review

Students will be responsible for:

1. A memory verse from one of the books that they studied during this unit, indicating the translation used and citing the reference.

2. The information included in the following SUPPLEMENTARY READINGS at the back of the student workbook:

   #14. "After the Exile: Overview"

   #17. "Self-Quiz: Mid-Unit Three"

   #20. "Self-Quiz: Unit Three Maps"

3. Identifying the historical order of major events in biblical history using the time-line of kings and prophets that they began in assignment I.2.

Suggested Lecture Topics

- Review the basic information about the biblical books studied in the third unit, stressing their historical context, theology, and major themes.
- Review the genre and structure of Hebrew poetry.
- Review the chronology of events covered in third year as well as the major events from years one and two.
- Review geography using the map quiz above.

Students express their appreciation for the members of their study group

The aim of this exercise is for students to express their appreciation for the members of their small group this year.

Each student:

1. Takes the name of one person in the small group. (Each group makes sure that all members have received a name; absent members should be contacted.)

2. Writes a brief testimonial about the gift that person's presence has been to the group during this year. Perhaps a guideline could be this message from Paul to the Ephesians (4:25–32 in part):

   > *So then, putting away falsehood, let all of us speak the truth to our neighbors, for we are members of one another... Let no evil talk come out of your mouths, but only what is useful for building up, as there is need, so that your words may give grace to those who hear... and be kind to one another, tenderhearted, forgiving one another, as God in Christ has forgiven you.*

3. Brings the testimonial the following week, shares it with the group, and then presents it to the person about whom he or she wrote.

Since students will be in different groups next year, they should reflect on the fact that new insights about their faith journey this year have come not only from their personal study but also from working together in their group week after week. They should also take to heart the words of the U.S. bishops' letter on evangelization, *Go and Make Disciples* (1992):

> *Conversion is the change of our lives which comes about through the power of the Holy Spirit. All who accept the Gospel undergo a change as we continually put on the mind of Christ by rejecting sin and becoming more faithful disciples in the church. Unless we undergo conversion, we have not truly accepted the Gospel.*

YEAR THREE
UNIT THREE TEST

Name ______________________________

Center ________________ **Group #** _____

1. Arrange the following events in chronological order.

David is crowned king	Kingdom is divided into Israel and Judah
Rebuilding of the temple	Conquest of the land of Canaan
Birth of Jesus	Missions of Ezra and Nehemiah
Exodus from Egypt	Jerusalem is destroyed by Babylon
Return of the exiles from Babylon	Northern Kingdom falls to Assyria

a. ______________________ f. ______________________

b. ______________________ g. ______________________

c. ______________________ h. ______________________

d. ______________________ i. ______________________

e. ______________________ j. ______________________

2. The psalms may be divided into a variety of categories/types. Name three of these categories/types and briefly describe the major characteristics of *one* of your choices.

3. Identify the type of parallelism found in each of the following couplets.

S (synonymous parallelism) A (antithetic parallelism)

_______ a. Then Israel came to Egypt,
Jacob lived as an alien in the land of Ham. (Ps 105:23)

_______ b. He does not deal with us according to our sins,
nor repay us according to our iniquities. (Ps 103:10)

_______ c. Many bulls encircle me,
strong bulls of Bashan surround me. (Ps 22:12)

_______ d. For you deliver a humble people,
but the haughty eyes you bring down. (Ps 18:27)

_______ e. For I was blameless before him,
and I kept myself from guilt. (Ps 18:23)

_______ f. I have become a stranger to my kindred
an alien to my mother's children. (Ps 69:8)

_______ g. For the LORD watches over the way of the righteous,
but the way of the wicked will perish. (Ps 1:6)

4. Write your memory verse from this unit. Be sure to give the book, chapter, verse, and translation used.

5. In the blank before each statement, write the name of the book (use Chronicles to refer to both books) that is best described by the statement.

Chronicles, Malachi, Joel, Deutero-Zechariah, Ruth, Song of Solomon (Song of Songs), Psalms

_______________ a. story of ancestor of David

_______________ b. locust plague as sign of the Day of the LORD

_______________ c. idealized David

_______________ d. hymnbook of the second temple

_______________ e. return of Elijah promised

_______________ f. celebration of human and divine love

_______________ g. reinterpretation of history to meet the needs of the post-exilic community

_______________ h. sees the outpouring of the spirit as one of the signs of the Day of the LORD

_______________ i. title of the book means "my messenger"

_______________ j. often interpreted in an allegorical way by both Jews and Christians

_______________ k. stresses immediate retribution

_______________ l. uses teaching dialogues

_______________ m. is very open to foreigners

_______________ n. focuses on the importance of ritual, temple worship, and the role of the Levites

_______________ o. a collection of poetic prayers expressing the human response to God

_______________ p. announces a king coming into Jerusalem on a donkey

6. What was your most significant learning experience during this unit's study?

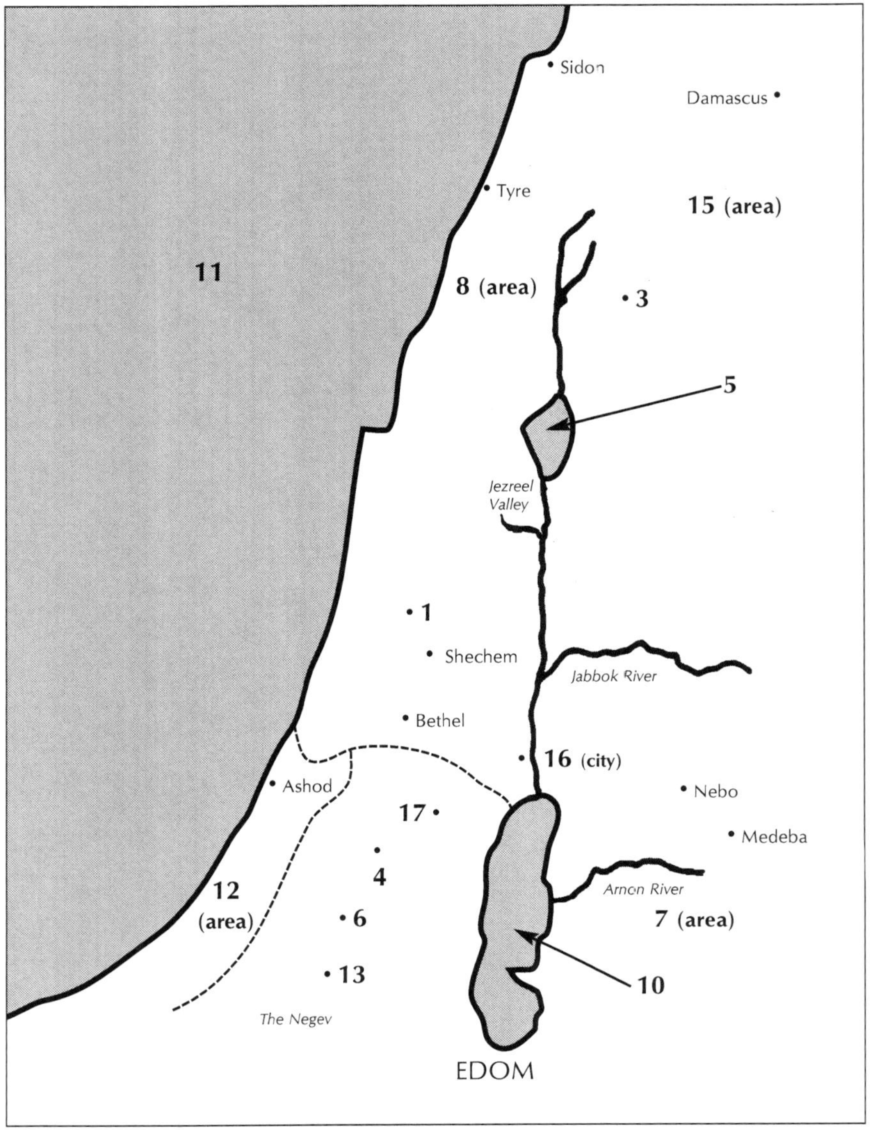

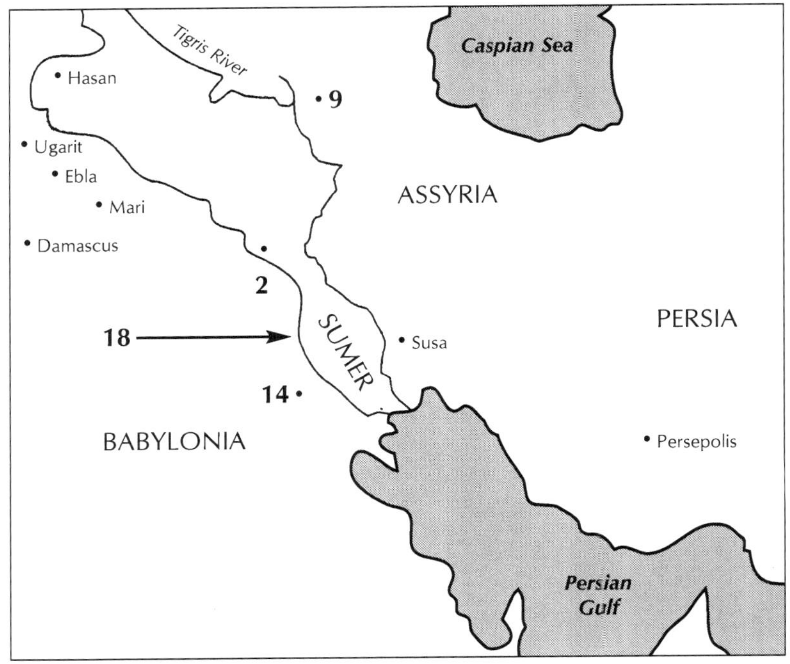

7. Map Test

_____ a. Babylon
_____ b. Beersheba
_____ c. Bethlehem
_____ d. Dan
_____ e. Dead Sea
_____ f. Euphrates River
_____ g. Hebron
_____ h. Jericho
_____ i. Jerusalem
_____ j. Mediterranean Sea
_____ k. Moab
_____ l. Nineveh
_____ m. Philistia
_____ n. Phoenicia
_____ o. Samaria (city)
_____ p. Sea of Galilee
_____ q. Syria
_____ r. Ur

ANSWERS TO YEAR THREE–UNIT THREE TEST

1. Chronology

a. Exodus from Egypt
b. Conquest of the land of Canaan
c. David is crowned king
d. Kingdom is divided into Israel and Judah
e. Northern Kingdom falls to Assyria
f. Jerusalem is destroyed by Babylon
g. Return of the exiles from Babylon
h. Rebuilding of the temple after the exile
i. Missions of Ezra and Nehemiah
j. Birth of Jesus

2. Some categories are: lament, praise, thanksgiving, confidence, royal, wisdom.

3. Types of Parallelism

a. S
b. S
c. S
d. A
e. S
f. S
g. A

5. Matching Books with Descriptions

a. Ruth
b. Joel
c. Chronicles
d. Psalms
e. Malachi
f. Song of Solomon (Song of Songs)
g. Chronicles
h. Joel
i. Malachi
j. Song of Solomon (Song of Songs)
k. Chronicles
l. Malachi
m. Ruth
n. Chronicles
o. Psalms
p. Deutero-Zechariah

7. Map Test

a. 2
b. 13
c. 4
d. 3
e. 10
f. 18
g. 6
h. 16
i. 17
j. 11
k. 7
l. 9
m. 12
n. 8
o. 1
p. 5
q. 15
r. 14

FOUR-YEAR PLAN OF STUDY IN THE CATHOLIC BIBLICAL SCHOOL

UNITS	BIBLICAL BOOKS	THEOLOGICAL THEMES	GENERAL ISSUES
FIRST YEAR: OLD TESTAMENT FOUNDATIONS — GENESIS THROUGH KINGS			
UNIT 1	Exodus Leviticus Numbers	People of God Covenant Desert	Sources of the Pentateuch
UNIT 2	Deuteronomy Genesis	Promise/The Land Creation/Sin	Form Criticism Fertile Crescent
UNIT 3	Joshua Judges 1 and 2 Samuel 1 and 2 Kings	Charismatic Leadership Kingship Prophecy	Geography of Palestine Canaanite Religion Biblical Chronology Biblical Archeology
SECOND YEAR: NEW TESTAMENT FOUNDATIONS — JESUS AND DISCIPLESHIP			
UNIT 1	Mark Luke Matthew 1 and 2	Discipleship Holy Spirit Infancy Narratives	Synoptic Question Form Criticism Redaction Criticism
UNIT 2	Acts Pauline Letters	Church Gifts of the Holy Spirit	New Testament Geography Letter as Literary Form
UNIT 3	John and Johannine Letters Mark 13, Luke 21 Matthew 24—25 Revelation	Sacraments Eschatology	Apocalyptic Writing
THIRD YEAR: OLD TESTAMENT CONTINUED — EXILE AND RESTORATION			
UNIT 1	Amos Hosea 1 Isaiah Micah Zephaniah Nahum Jeremiah	Social Justice Prophetic Vocation Marriage of God and Israel	Biblical Chronology
UNIT 2	Lamentations Obadiah Ezekiel 2 Isaiah Haggai Zechariah 1—8 3 Isaiah Ezra Nehemiah	Destruction of the Temple Meaning of the Exile Renewal after Exile Community Rebuilt around the Word	Crisis of the Exile Strategies of Renewal
UNIT 3	1 and 2 Chronicles Joel Malachi Zechariah 9–14 Ruth Song of Songs Psalms	Rebuilding a People Importance of the Law	Historical Writings of Old Testament Hebrew Poetry Jewish Liturgy
FOURTH YEAR: BOTH TESTAMENTS CONCLUDED — THE WORD IN THE HELLENISTIC WORLD			
UNIT 1	Proverbs Habakkuk Job Ecclesiastes Sirach Wisdom	Creation Emphasis Problem of Suffering	Priest, Prophet, and Sage
UNIT 2	Jonah Esther Tobit Baruch 1 and 2 Maccabees Judith Daniel	Martyrdom Resurrection	Deuterocanonical Books Hellenism
UNIT 3	Matthew Pastoral Letters Catholic Letters Hebrews	Role of Peter/Apostles New Testament as Fulfillment of Old Testament	Christianity as a New Form of Religion in the Roman World